C000084740

Becoming NEET

For loving parents Anthony and Cheryl – for their endless support –
and to dear Mark, Toby, and Jo, who continue to inspire.

Becoming NEET

Risks, rewards, and realities

Christopher Arnold and Tracey Baker

A Trentham Book
Institute of Education Press

First published in 2013 by the Institute of Education, University of London,
20 Bedford Way, London WC1H 0AL
www.ioe.ac.uk/ioepress

© Christopher Arnold and Tracey Baker 2013

British Library Cataloguing in Publication Data:
A catalogue record for this publication is available from the British Library

ISBNs
978-1-85856-524-8 (paperback)
978-1-85856-531-6 (PDF eBook)
978-1-85856-532-3 (ePub eBook)
978-1-85856-533-0 (Kindle eBook)

All rights reserved. No part of this publication may be reproduced, stored in a
retrieval system, or transmitted in any form or by any means, electronic, mechanical,
photocopying, recording or otherwise, without the prior permission of the
copyright owner.

Every effort has been made to trace copyright holders and to obtain their permission
for the use of copyright material. The publisher apologizes for any errors or omissions
and would be grateful if notified of any corrections that should be incorporated in
future reprints or editions of this book.

The opinions expressed in this publication are those of the authors and do not
necessarily reflect the views of the Institute of Education, University of London.

Typeset by Quadrant Infotech (India) Pvt Ltd
Printed by CPI Group (UK) Ltd, Croydon, CR0 4YY

Contents

List of figures and tables

Acknowledgements

We are deeply indebted to many people for their support for this book: Ana Aparicio and Kathy Ross for their contributions to Chapter 4; Ed Dales and Chris Latham for their constructive criticism of early drafts; Ro Hands from the Learnplay Foundation for her help identifying suitable case studies; Myia Khela for her assistance with transcription; Peter Holtham for his continued support from Connexions; Andrew Gravenstede and Kevin Rowland for recognizing the relevance to Inclusion Support; Joanna Caveney for her heroic work on an earlier draft; Gillian Klein for her patience; our many colleagues in Connexions Sandwell and Inclusion Support who have suffered persistent questioning; and finally, Sylvia, for her good humour.

About the authors

Christopher Arnold is an educational psychologist who has worked in the West Midlands for more than a quarter of a century. In addition to the usual work of a local authority psychologist he has researched and written in a range of areas including applying psychology to the work of teaching assistants, breakfast clubs, exclusion, and inclusive practice as well as those young people not in education, employment, or training. His publications include: *Psychology for Teaching Assistants*; *Teaching, Learning and Psychology*; *Excluded from School: Complex discourses and psychological perspectives*; *Italy's Alternatives to Exclusion*; and a number of journal papers. He has collaborated with Tracey Baker for a number of years in developing screening tools to identify vulnerable young people in order to facilitate early intervention. He was chair of the British Psychological Society's Division for Educational and Child Psychology in 2012.

Tracey Baker graduated from the University of Birmingham in 2002 with a BSC in Psychology and Sports Science. Her dissertation work was subsequently published in *Nature Neuroscience* as 'Seeing the action: Neuropsychological evidence for action-based effects on object selection'. After a short time working in the health and fitness industry she moved into her current Connexions Personal Adviser role providing impartial information, advice, guidance, and support for young people in their post-16 transition. She has been involved in a NEET prevention screening project alongside Christopher Arnold throughout her time at Connexions, which has developed her role to include mentoring and consultancy. Publications resulting from this work include the papers 'Developing a NEET screening tool' and 'Transitions from school to work: Applying psychology to "NEET"'. She plays badminton at both local and national level as well as coaching younger players to achieve their potential.

Chapter 1

The risks

NEET is a relatively recent term used to describe young people who leave statutory education and do not engage in further education, employment, or training. It first appeared in 1999 from the UK Government's Social Exclusion Unit and is increasingly being found in government documents and news items. While the term may be new, the phenomenon is not; studies of youth unemployment have been undertaken for decades. As Robson (2008) pointed out, the interest is not simply in young people not engaging in education, employment, or training, but in the consequences of this inactivity 'occupying an unconstructive (and potentially threatening) position in the social topography'. For the purposes of this book we will not be restricting the term to 16-year-olds. Instead we refer to young people who do not engage in education, employment, or training. Despite changes in legislation that might see a proportion of 16- or 17-year-olds continuing with some sort of training, the trend of young people who may be 16 or over not engaging in any post-statutory activity is likely to continue. Those who are NEET are seen as a drain on society, rather than people whose situations are extremely varied and often problematic. Whatever the starting assumptions, the risks and outcomes for this group are a matter of concern:

- national figures from 2009 showed that 183,200 young people (9.2 per cent) of young people aged 16–18 were NEET
- over their lifetimes the 2008 NEET cohort will cost an estimated £13 billion in public finance and £22 billion in opportunity expenses
- compared to their peers young men who were NEET are three times more likely to suffer from depression and five times more likely to have a criminal record
- data from fieldwork areas found that a quarter of young people were NEET at some point during a two-year period, but most get into education, employment, or training (although 10 per cent remain NEET for six months or more)
- while national NEET levels have fluctuated between 9 and 10 per cent for 20 years, this statistic disguises wider variations:
  o local NEET levels range from 2 to 14 per cent
  o 18-year-olds are more likely to be NEET (17 per cent) than 16-year-olds (4 per cent)

- many areas have reduced NEET levels among 16–18-year-olds, but there is less success in tackling the increase in unemployment for those aged 18–24 (Audit Commission, 2010).

More recent work suggests that the incidence is increasing:

Table 1.1: NEET rates for different age cohorts

	Quarter 2, 2009	Quarter 2, 2010	Quarter 2, 2011	% change from 2010 to 2011
Age 16	8.0%	4.9%	6.3%	1.4
Age 17	11.2%	10.2%	8.8%	-1.3
Age 18	16.5%	15.0%	14.3%	-0.8
Age 16–18	11.9%	10.2%	9.8%	-0.3
Age 19–24	17.8%	16.5%	19.1%	2.6
Age 16–24	15.9%	14.4%	16.2%	1.7

And has been increasing steadily for a long time:

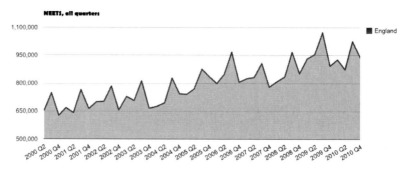

Figure 1.1: NEET figures 2000–10

The realities for this group are stark. Research by Bynner and Parsons (2002) showed that young males had very poor labour experiences, while the majority of young women were teenage mothers, many of whom had mental health problems, particularly depression and low self-esteem. Later research by Maguire and Rennison (2005) looked at the failure of government schemes to engage this group. It concluded that many had disengaged from education because they were excluded, bullied, had poor skills, or were simply uninterested, which made engagement with such schemes unlikely.

The outcomes for young men are particularly worrying. They are:

- four times more likely to be unemployed
- five times more likely to have a criminal record

- six times more likely to have poor qualifications and lower potential earnings and tax contributions
- three times more likely to have mental health problems such as depression, which incurs an additional cost to the National Health Service (Audit Commission, 2010).

If we consider two different sums – lost income to the treasury from tax and national insurance (opportunity costs) and the more explicit costs of various benefits (public finance costs) – the strain on the public purse is staggering (Audit Commission, 2010):

Table 1.2: Costs of NEET young people

Age range	Opportunity costs	Public finance costs
Short term (16–18)	£2 billion	£2 billion
Medium term (19–59)	£20 billion	£11 billion
Long term (60 and over)	–	< £1 billion
Total	£22 billion	> £13 billion

International studies support the view that entering the NEET category leads to poorer life outcomes. A study in Sweden found that economic inactivity among adults in their early 20s was likely to persist for a minimum of seven years (Franzen and Kassman, 2005). Comparing countries across Europe meanwhile, Walther and Pohl (2005) found that those with high numbers of young people who were NEET were characterized by ineligibility for benefits, a sense of abandonment, and an informal economy. Low educational levels was an evident factor and poverty was the common denominator.

People living in long-term poverty have poorer health outcomes:

- in England and Wales life expectancy varies between the lowest and highest social classes: on average, wealthy men live 7.4 years longer than those living in poverty; for women, the difference is an average of 4.2 years (Office for National Statistics, 2011:10)
- men from the poorest income groups are twice as likely to die prematurely as those from the managerial and professional groups (Office for National Statistics, 2011:24)
- the incidence of mental illness in the poorest group is twice that of the most affluent (Health and Social Care Information Centre, 2011)
- for people who are unemployed or in low-paid jobs the incidence of life-limiting and long-standing illness or disability is more than twice

as high as for those in the highest social classes (Office for National Statistics, 2011).

More recent work suggests that such negative effects can often endure. Uzuki (2010) has researched the risk of long-term intergenerational poverty for those entering the NEET category. If a 16-year-old male from a family classified as poor enters the NEET category, he is 70 per cent more likely to remain poor in the long term. If the same 16-year-old enters employment, but goes on to lose the position and become unemployed, risk of long-term poverty is reduced to 40 per cent. This statistic does not hold for young women. There is no difference in the risk of long-term intergenerational poverty between women who enter the NEET category when they are 16 and women who enter employment. If we are working to increase social mobility then it is worthwhile targeting young people in statutory education to ensure that they have some experience of work.

While the term NEET might suggest a homogeneous category, evidence from various studies highlights different sub-groups. The Youth Cohort Study data from Spielhofer *et al.* (2009) in the Learning and Skills Network (LSN) report describes three:

- open to learning (41 per cent): this group has positive attitudes towards future learning, but has become NEET as a result of some poor choices in education. They are optimistic about future job prospects
- undecided (22 per cent): these students have negative attitudes towards education and are unable to make up their minds as to what to do next. Sixty per cent of this group were still in the NEET category after one year, twice as many as in the previous group
- sustained (38 per cent): the young people in this group tend to come from complex and sometimes chaotic backgrounds. They have negative experiences of school and 60 per cent remain in the NEET category after one year.

Other groups who would be classified as NEET include the following: young people who choose gap years before going on to further or higher education; young parents who choose to care for their children; and young people whose parents are particularly wealthy and who can therefore support them if they choose not to engage.

Within these groups there is still considerable regional, national, and international variation. In 2007 the lowest and highest incidences were in Torbay (0.8 per cent) and North Lincolnshire (22 per cent) respectively. The LSN report (2009) highlights that the circumstances leading to NEET status are often rooted in local factors, while the report examining differences across Europe (Robson, 2008) arrives at a somewhat surprising conclusion: of the wide range of possible factors there were no systematic differences by regime type in predictors or outcomes for those with NEET status. In the UK only four factors offered any predictive validity: sex, age, middle quintile of income, and bottom quintile of income. The author pointed out the absence in this study of many of the factors found in previous studies: parental education, truancy, bullying, learning difficulties, or physical characteristics of the environment.

There is a significant difference between the studies. Robson's involves expansive populations while the others tend to draw data from local groups. The presence of these factors in the smaller studies supports the proposition that local factors are involved. The international studies, though thoroughly extensive, tend to average out local factors, often obscuring the detail that highlights what leads a person into the NEET category. As this book shows, if we take into account the fact that there are differences across communities and in habits, as well as the use of family networks and attitudes towards benefits, work, and training, then greater understanding can be gained by examining the individuals in a community. While large studies can provide valuable insights into the macro-economics of NEET, they might miss important and useable information at the individual and community levels.

Some common features can be found, particularly when looking at a local level. We describe these as risk factors that themselves have common elements. Wilson *et al.* (2008) highlighted the nature of the transition between education and work. They describe the 'non-linear pathways' traced by some young people and are critical of analyses that focus on the already identified vulnerable groups, such as those leaving the care system. By starting from concern about such groups, the detail of personal circumstances can be disregarded and large numbers of NEET young people who are not members of these easily identified groups can be missed.

National studies have identified possible risk factors (Audit Commission, 2010):

Table 1.3: Identified NEET risk factors

Risk factor	Increase in likelihood of being NEET for at least six months
Previous experience of being NEET	7.9 times more likely
Pregnancy or parenthood	2.8 times more likely

Risk factor	Increase in likelihood of being NEET for at least six months
Supervision by youth offending team	2.6 times more likely
Fewer than three months in post-16 education	2.3 times more likely
Disclosed substance abuse	2.1 times more likely
Responsibilities as a carer	2.0 times more likely

We suggest that similar risk factors are present in the following scenarios and possibly more:

- being excluded from school
- having mental health problems
- not being in education, employment, or training at 16 or 17.

There are similarities with heart attack risk factors.

Consider the following tables:

Table 1.4: Factors associated with permanent exclusion: Incidence of destabilizing factors in 31 pupils who were permanently excluded from school

Factor	Incidence
Mental health problems	8
Special educational needs (SEN)	14
Looked after children (LAC)	1
Single parent	11
Disabled parent	5
Domestic violence	8
Parental rejection	14
Parental substance misuse	4
Parental mental health problems	4
Parental reports of behaviour management problems	18
Child Protection Register	8
No fixed abode/rough sleeping	4
Risk of sexual exploitation	3

Pitchford's 2006 study showed that children with five or more factors in their lives were more likely to be permanently excluded from school. Arnold *et al.* (2009) demonstrated the link between instability in children's lives and the kinds of behaviour that often result in children being excluded from school.

Mental health problems are also associated with instability. The National Children's Home (NCH) study (2007) has identified the following factors as being significant in their development:

Table 1.5: Factors associated with mental health risk problems

Within child	Within family	Within community
Specific learning difficulties	Overt parental conflict	Socio-economic disadvantage
Communication difficulties	Family breakdown	Homelessness
Specific developmental delay	Inconsistent or unclear discipline	Disaster
Genetic influence	Hostile or rejecting relationships	Discrimination
Difficult temperament	Failure to adapt to child's changing needs	Other significant life events
Physical illness especially if chronic and/or neurological	Physical, sexual, or emotional abuse	
Academic failure	Parent psychiatric illness	
Low self-esteem	Parental criminality, alcoholism, or personality disorder	
	Death and loss – including loss of friendship	

source: NCH, 2007.

Let us now consider factors associated with entering the NEET category:

Table 1.6: Factors associated with NEET

Unstable accommodation
Low motivation (no idea of what to do after statutory school leaving)
A history of poor behaviour in school
Unemployment in family
Poor basic skills
Involvement with the youth offending team
School attendance < 80%
Categorized as having a Learning Difficulty or Disability (LDD)

source: Arnold and Baker, 2011.

If we look at the tables together, poor basic skills, difficulties in parenting and domestic instability are common across all three. We suggest that while there might be differences in certain details, these reflect the nature of the studies from which the findings come rather than anything significant. We also emphasize the common feature of *instability,* which can be found in the tables for heart attack risk factors:

Table 1.7: Holmes and Rahe's social readjustment rating scale

Factor	Weighting
Death of spouse	100
Divorce	73
Marital separation	65
Jail term	63
Death of close family member	63
Personal injury or illness	53
Marriage	50
Fired at work	47
Marital reconciliation	45
Retirement	45
Change in health of family member	44
Pregnancy	40
Sexual difficulties	39
Gain of new family member	39
Business readjustment	39
Change in financial state	38
Death of close friend	37
Change of different line of work	36
Change in number of arguments with	35
spouse	31
Large mortgage	30
Foreclosure of mortgage or loan	29
Change in responsibilities at work	29
Son or daughter leaving home	29
Trouble with in-laws	28
Outstanding personal achievement	26
Spouse begins or stops work	26
Beginning or ending school	25
Change in living conditions	24

Factor	Weighting
Revision of personal habits	23
Trouble with boss	20
Change in work hours or conditions	20
Change in residence	20
Change in school	19
Change in recreation	19
Change in church activities	18
Change in social activities	17
Middle size mortgage	16
Change in sleeping habits	15
Change in number of family get-togethers	15
Change in eating habits	13
Holidays	12
Christmas	12
Minor violations of the law	11

source: Holmes and Rahe, 1967.

When looking at instability and change, poor outcomes in education, employment, mental health, and physical health appear significant determinants. It is possible that stress is a common mediating factor.

The Holmes and Rahe table introduces a new dimension: the additive nature of each risk factor. If we think of this table as describing stress factors, we see a cumulative effect when more than one is present. We suggest that each factor we have highlighted carries some potential to cause change or instability and therefore some degree of stress. Such instability – and the associated stress – makes people more susceptible to being excluded from school, experiencing mental health problems, being in poorer health, and entering the NEET category, and while other studies in this area have made similar propositions (Audit Commission, 2010), none has been explored in any depth. If the case for examining local factors is accepted, it seems likely that any cumulative effects might also reflect local conditions.

It is this that forms the nature of our particular enquiry. Two contrasting but complementary approaches to studying the phenomenon of NEET are available. On the one hand there are widespread studies that cover large populations. These have the advantage of gathering information across a range of contexts and communities. On the other are smaller, locally based studies that focus on the distinctive characteristics found in local communities.

Those working at a local level must adopt the same rigour applied in large-scale studies and must capture the experience and meaning for the individuals involved. By considering both, we hope to generate insights that will lead to improvements in interventions.

Our understanding of how instability impacts on people's lives has increased over recent decades. By conceptualizing challenging behaviour as a reasonable response to instability, we can change the ways that certain young people are perceived. Consider as an example the following situation: a teenage girl refuses to take her leather jacket off in a science lesson. The school rule is clear: jackets should be removed. The girl is adamant that she is not going to comply. At first glance, the girl might be seen as defiantly threatening the school's authority. A possible consequence for her might be some kind of corrective measure. Perhaps she would be required to stay after school in a detention; perhaps she would be sent home; perhaps her parents would be called. What happened was that a member of the pastoral staff in the school explored what the problem might be. The member of staff learned that she was homeless and sleeping on friends' sofas – 'sofa cruising'. She had difficulty getting her clothes clean, but was fastidious about her appearance. To remove her jacket would have revealed untidy clothing, something she felt very insecure about, particularly in front of her peers. By understanding the context she was living in and by seeing her response as reasonable if viewed from a different perspective, we might change our responses to other young people.

A framework that assists us in this type of analysis has been used successfully to reduce both exclusions from school and the incidence of NEET in vulnerable groups. The term 'chaos theory', borrowed from a field of mathematics, is often misrepresented. It is not a method of conceptualizing random events or phenomena but a way of finding systematic patterns in complex situations, to which, in the field of social sciences, it also makes suggestions for facilitating change in them.

According to Arnold *et al.* (2009) features of chaotic systems include:

- children changing their behaviour quite quickly
- apparently insignificant events becoming highly significant later on
- things appearing to be going well for a time, but then to change quickly
- the impossibility of predicting (anticipating) beyond the immediate future
- the absence of a full analysis – each level of explanation can be added to. You never get 'the full story'
- signals evident just before something big happens and things taking a little time to calm down following a big change.

For those working with young people in school such features will be familiar.

Non-linear development will inevitably occur under the following conditions. When:

- the learning process is iterative: the output from one learning cycle acts as the input for the next
- at least three (but ideally many more) items or options are competing for the attention of the learner
- the learner's attention is a finite commodity: attending to (or learning) one thing means that less attention can be given to another
- there are no large-scale, predetermined forces or architectures that determine what is learned (ibid.).

The last point is debatable. As we show in this book, some young people's family circumstances might predispose them to enter the NEET category.

Certain features are common across all chaotic systems. These include (ibid.):

- sudden jumps and changes in children's learning and behaviour
- delayed effects of different kinds of teaching and experiences
- variation in uncertainty in the course of development; there will be times when learning and behaviour appear steady and almost linear and other times when they might appear almost random
- a limit to the extent to which future learning and behaviour can be predicted – the term 'prediction horizon' has been used to describe this
- at each level of analysis more detail becomes visible
- there will be greater variability in behaviour before and after a sudden change in the child's situation; these 'chaotic markers' can signal that such a change is imminent.

Among the young people who enter the NEET category the incidence of instability is high. The features we have outlined are the inevitable consequences that translate into several contemporary problems, many of which are challenging for the professionals working in these areas.

Change need not be gradual. Young people might alter their habits quickly and unpredictably. Such changes might result from certain experiences that occurred some time before. Young people might appear stable for a while and then suddenly show signs of instability. Periods of calm might be swiftly followed by periods of intensive chaos. It can be impossible to predict events beyond the immediate future. A student who is reliable at attending school, or appointments, could suddenly withdraw; others, conversely, might start to co-operate. When you ask about the lives they lead, their accounts become more and more complex. There is always more that may be learned about what their lives are like. Finally, when change does occur, for example when leaving statutory education, there will be greater instability either side of the transition than usual. When considering the level of instability for children in Key Stage 4 (aged 15 or 16) it is likely to be higher than they have previously experienced or will do in the future.

If we are right about the role instability plays in young people entering the NEET category there are ways we can both improve services and avoid making them less effective.

Young people with unstable lives can have a multiplicity of professionals involved with them: teachers, pastoral support managers, learning mentors, Connexions workers, social workers, Child and Adolescent Mental Health Services (CAMHS) staff, educational psychologists, behaviour support staff, police officers, and youth offending team staff. The list could continue. Among such professionals there might be different expectations and conflicting ideas about promoting the young person's best interests. Young people are asked to form relationships with these adults, whose different agendas can inadvertently lead to greater instability and its associated consequences. If a young person tries to avoid contact with as many of these adults as possible, they are often described as being hard to reach.

The agencies employing such professionals are likely to have to report on their performance, which is usually evaluated against successful outcomes typically measured in observable terms. For those who need to justify their funding – or are competing with other agencies – it can be difficult to argue that continued attempts to engage with hard to reach young clients are worth it. Schools have influenced their data about examination successes if they have convinced students and their families who are unlikely to do well to move away. Some actively encourage families to educate their children at home so they can remove the child's results from those they need to declare. For a more detailed account of the lengths to which schools will go, see Syke (2010).

The pressures that agencies are under to report positive outcomes can lead to dangerous practices. Once again, they increase how much instability a young person experiences. If young people are offered appointments but fail to attend they can be discharged from the service, despite the fact that failing to attend might signal a greater need for support. The sheer number of agencies available for young people might lead to processes described by Arnold *et al.* (2009) as 'pass the parcel' and 'the agency game'.

If we speak to a group of people who have knowledge of the same events it is not uncommon for them to provide different stories and accounts. When working with people in unstable situations, additional elements need to be taken into consideration. Ross (1977) developed the concept of *fundamental attribution error* to describe the tendency for an individual to externalize the reasons for a negative outcome more than people observing the events do. In other words, an observer is more likely to attribute blame for a negative event to a person than the person themselves. For example, if a person loses a job they are more likely to blame another person or factors; they might think, 'It was the manager – he never liked me,' or, 'It's the economy; there's no work out there.' Observers might attribute the outcome to the manager's action, however, they might think, 'It was your fault – you should never have insulted the manager,' or, 'You needed to work hard to maintain the job and you chose to slack.' If this is the case, trying to understand the situation from a single perspective is unlikely to be useful if gaining a full picture or the desired outcome: the situation needs to be interpreted from multiple perspectives. Consider the circumstances of a young person who has just left school and is not engaged with education, employment, or training. A number of people are likely to be involved with promoting their best interests, including:

- Connexions personal adviser
- parent
- school
- potential provider of education, employment, or training
- the person concerned.

There may also be others. To gain a comprehensive picture of the situation and how to improve it each of the professionals would be required to provide their accounts. While such information gathering is regrettably rare, it is extremely useful when analysing the situations that cause people to become NEET.

A further factor that leads to instability is the lack of large-scale plans or architecture: an absence of robust and predetermined pathways for young people that we consider positive. If an entire household is economically inactive and the youngest child sees staying at home on benefits as an inevitable consequence we might consider this outcome a reflection of a large-scale plan. The professionals involved with the young person, however, would be unlikely to share any particular aspiration. So though we recognize that for some young people no outcome is possible, we assert that the professionals involved with them would reject it in favour of others.

Building robust plans for individuals living unstable lives is not easy. A common tendency is to widen their range of support – and thus increase the level of instability. An alternative approach might restrict the contact to one professional only who works with the individual for an extended period of time. If the professional has access to all the relevant information and support, the approach might be more conducive to increasing the individual's level of stability – and therefore reduce the likelihood of there being negative outcomes. For this to happen it is imperative that the professional works with the individual through the transition from leaving statutory education, undertaking additional education, moving on to a training course or moving into employment. Being a stable and consistent presence in the individual's life is central if they are to reduce the chance of the person remaining NEET long term.

Conclusion

We consider that the phenomenon of NEET is a negative force for those it characterizes.

For young people whose lives have many sources of instability, the likelihood of entering the NEET category is higher than it is for others.

Understanding the instability in young people's lives requires multiple perspectives and accounts.

Certain interventions can inadvertently increase the level of instability that a young person experiences.

Building stable support systems could require different approaches from those that are currently adopted.

This book examines these particular considerations. It starts by investigating two strands that underpin our current thinking: the history of childhood – and how long it lasts – and the history of employment.

Chapter 2

A history of childhood

Introduction

Behind our concern for young people who are NEET are two histories: employment and our images of childhood. To understand this concern, we can gain certain insights from our past beliefs and actions about what constitutes childhood, including opinions about what young people *ought* to be like and what they *ought* to do. Such ideas have been transformed throughout history and by studying these beliefs and how they have changed we can understand our concerns in a number of different ways.

We contextualize the phenomenon NEET in the transition from childhood to adulthood, territories defined not only by age but by roles and functions. In this chapter we consider the rapidly changing nature of childhood roles and consider them in the context of changes over a longer history.

To understand the significance of our interest in the NEET cohort, it is useful to examine the ages and stages – between which there is considerable variation – at which young people are considered to be independent from their families. This will need to include the nature of childhood, adulthood, and employment and how these definitions have changed over time.

The nature of childhood

In the last 30 years the concept of childhood – as a phase of life distinct from adulthood – has attracted a degree of attention (Aries, 1960; deMause, 1974; Postman, 1994; Heywood, 2001; Cunningham, 2006). Throughout history its nature and definition have varied significantly according to various factors, which have been accounted for by a number of alternative models and theories. This chapter highlights what factors are relevant to understanding the transition from childhood, or perhaps adolescence, to adulthood.

Nowadays we might have the following conception of childhood: a phase in which adults protect, nurture, and promote from birth the development of young people until they consider themselves adults and are able to do such things for themselves. Childhood has not always been a safe time for children, however. Euripides wrote of widespread infanticide, particularly for children who were seen as less than perfect:

Children were thrown into rivers, flung into dung-heaps and cess trenches, 'potted' in jars to starve to death and exposed on every hill and roadside, a prey for birds, food for wild beasts to rend. To begin with, any child that was not perfect in shape and size, or cried too little or too much, or was otherwise than is described in the gynaecological writings on *How to Recognise the Newborn that is Worth Rearing* was generally killed.

(deMause, 1974: 25)

Exposure was a method of infanticide that Seneca justified with apparent ease:

Mad dogs we knock on the head; the fierce and savage ox we slay; sickly sheep we put to the knife to keep them from infecting the flock; unnatural progeny we destroy; we drown even children who at birth are weakly and abnormal. Yet it is not anger but reason that separates the harmful from the sound.

(ibid.: 27)

But abnormality – in any form – was not the only reason for infanticide. As this instruction by Hilarion to his wife Alis in 1 BC shows, girls were less valued than boys: 'If, as may well happen, you give birth to a child, if it is a boy, let it live; if it is a girl, expose it.' (ibid.: 26). Such practices led to large gender imbalances in certain populations. One is recorded in Milesia around 220 BC where there were 118 boys and just 28 girls. Evidence suggests that selection by gender had been the practice since prehistoric times. A study of fossils from the Mesolithic era found that the sex ratio of males to females was 148 to 100 (Vallois, cited in deMause, 1974), while an examination of church records suggests that the practice continued for centuries with ratios standing at 156 to 100 in AD 801 and 172 to 100 in 1391.

Being of the wrong gender was not the only hazard of early life; child sacrifice was also common. The practice found in Jericho in biblical times – sealing children in walls to ensure their strength – was common in many other cultures and endured until 1843, when the last incidence was recorded in Germany (Darlington, 1931). Using children as suicide bombers in contemporary conflicts reminds us that for some, childhood is not as safe a time as we would like to imagine.

Those condemning such practices have existed since ancient times, too. In the Roman era there are accounts of disapproval and changes in the law. By AD 374 infanticide became the crime of murder and by 787 institutions were being developed to care for abandoned children. Some other figures involved are well known. In the fourth century AD Nicholas, bishop of Myra (now in Turkey), established institutions for the disabled and the poor. His name lives on as St Nicholas, the basis for the figure of Santa Claus. His influence extended as far as Belgium where he has been credited with founding an institution to care for the disabled.

Other institutions included the Pietà in Venice, which devised a measure to reduce the large number of newborns being abandoned in the city's canals. The institution provided a small hole (*scaffetta*) in a wall through which the baby could be 'posted'. If the parent waited too long, the baby would be too big to fit so the measure only worked for newborn babies. As the children grew up they were cared for and educated; the boys were sent out to work and the girls were trained in music. Much later, in 1741, philanthropist Tomas Coram opened an orphanage in London in response to seeing babies abandoned in the streets and dung heaps of the city. Even with this facility, dead and dying babies were still a commonplace in London until the end of the nineteenth century (deMause, 1974).

If death was avoided, other terrors lay in wait. The mutilation of children was permissible, particularly as an aid to begging. Seneca justified acts of mutilation – such as the breaking of limbs, the crushing of feet, blinding and even the removal of arms – if it meant receiving greater offerings from adults who were amused by the children's deformities. 'What wrong has been done to the republic? On the contrary, have not these children been done a service inasmuch as their parents have cast them out?' (deMause, 1974).

The idea of a child as a commodity that could be sold or traded led to a number of additional dangers. In the seventh century the Archbishop of Canterbury ruled that children could not be sold into slavery after the age of seven. For many centuries the age marked a point in potential transition from childhood into the world of work for those in the non-literate classes. As a consequence of such commodification, children could be offered as security for debts and kept as virtual hostages. When Henry I's son-in-law put out the eyes of one of his household, the king allowed the victim's father to mutilate another child in recompense. 'An eye for an eye' might have been an Old Testament rule but it endured for at least a thousand years.

Physical punishment was justified as discipline. In Sparta, flagellation contests could involve whipping children to death. Physical pain ensured that children remembered events more accurately. When they were used as witnesses in Anglo-Saxon legal proceedings, children would be flogged with unusual severity to increase the credibility of their statements. Records of recommendations in Renaissance times, meanwhile, provided instructions for adults on how to beat children to ensure they did not die: children were not to be hit around their heads and faces with instruments such as shovels or cudgels; rods were to be used to hit them on their sides so that they might learn instead. There are countless records of physical punishment given to children over time. It is less than one generation ago (1987) that physical punishment was still legal – and often used – within the countries of the European Union.

So childhood, for however long it lasted, was not always the safe place depicted in certain story books.

The duration of childhood

Defining the duration of childhood requires an understanding of its nature. How do we know if a person is a child – or adolescent – or adult? Many may recall the times when children dressed differently from adults: boys wore short trousers, girls wore school skirts. If we look at today's fashions, however, this distinguishing feature is hard to detect. Shops sell T-shirts for 7-year-old girls with inserts to suggest breasts. Jeans available for both sexes are identical to those made for young adults. Few children wear their hair in age-specific styles, such as ponytails and plaits. As Postman (1994) observed, it is only fairly recently that childhood has developed as a stage requiring different clothes and manners of behaving. Erasmus first suggested it, but it was not until the eighteenth century that it became widely accepted.

Far from being static throughout history, defining a young person as a child has depended on a number of factors. Postman (1994) proposed a framework suggesting that social class may account for the changes over time. Childhood, as a separate state from adulthood, requires society to have three elements: education, literacy, and shame.

In Roman times the first two elements were in evidence while the development of laws protecting children from harm suggested a sense of shame and perhaps compassion; adults had to protect children from the dangers that existed in adult life and of which they are ashamed. Postman (1994) suggested that childhood sees adults shielding children from their secrets, such as sexual desires, greed, and fear. With the end of the Roman Empire, literacy returned to the province of the few professional classes – such as those working in religion and law – where knowledge was transmitted by writing; for the rest, the oral tradition sufficed. The age at which most children were able to speak and understand was 7. This age set the boundary between children living in families without the need to work and young people embarking on apprenticeships, working in the fields, and in other ways becoming economically active members of the community:

> The 7-year-old male was a man in every respect except for his capacity to make love and war. Certainly, there was no separate world of childhood. Children shared the same games with adults, the same toys, the same fairy stories. They lived their lives together, never apart.
>
> (Postman, 1994)

By the time they were 7, young people had the skills to function in the adult world and contribute to it. Command over speech granted them access and they were at the age according to the Catholic Church where they were able to tell the difference between right and wrong.

When the printing press made writing widely available, the skills required for adult life changed. Mastering print became a valuable skill. Prior to this most 7-year-olds had no need for reading and writing; knowledge was transmitted orally, whether through sermons, stories, or apprenticeships. Print – and the need to master it – increased the length of time that children were dependent on adults to acquire the skills of the adult world – at least for those classes using it. It was not until the seventeenth century that Western European languages had words to define young males between 7 and about 15.

> The printing press created a new definition of adulthood *based on reading incompetence.* Prior to the coming of that new environment, infancy ended at 7 and adulthood began at once. There was no intervening stage because none was needed. That is why prior to the sixteenth century there were no books on child-rearing, and exceedingly few about women in their role as mothers.
>
> (Postman, 1994)

Though we might think of print as universal now, studies of present-day societies confirm that many remain illiterate. As recently as thirty years ago, Connell (1991) highlighted a Nepalese community in which neither print nor schooling were commonplace. Children were raised in families, but helped the economy of the family when tasks (usually agricultural) required it. The point at which a person stops being a child in such families is marked more by marriage than by work. Upon marrying, women leave the family home to live with the family of their new husband who continues his activities on the family's farm. Schooling and literacy are not seen as adding value, unless the family starts trading with other communities. In this society, adulthood is not a state that a child must attain, whereas in the literate society children become adults. Childhood is a separate state with its own rules and expectations, a state in which members are protected from some knowledge that only adults hold.

Adult shame as an element that defines childhood has been described by at least two writers: Postman and deMause. Adults seek to protect children from the realities of life they experience – but this has not always been the case. In the Middle Ages sexual activities with children were commonplace, knowledge of sexual acts was unconcealed, and sparing children from hearing offensive language was not considered necessary. As a new state of childhood emerged, however, one that served to protect young people from the realities of adult life so that they might learn the skills of reading and writing, a new sense of shame also developed. Since adults had certain forms of knowledge and behaved in ways that were not to be shared by children, childhood was extended.

By the eighteenth century writers like Rousseau were suggesting that children needed to be protected from sexual exploitation if they were to become virtuous adults. Childhood was a time for innocence, untainted by the unpleasant realities of life that characterized adulthood. Today our legal framework protects children from many situations that would have been quite acceptable in medieval times.

Such charity did not extend to all areas, however. Children were still seen as commodities to be traded and used for profit. In 1761 a woman was sentenced to a mere two years in jail for blinding children before sending them out begging. Far from being issued because of the injury to the children – the offence was the damaging of the property of others – the sentence reflected the fact that the children were not hers (Postman, 1994). Stealing a child was not an offence until 1814. Children were treated as adults by the law and if young people committed crimes that warranted the death penalty, they could pay the ultimate price. In 1808 a 7-year-old girl was sentenced to death by hanging in Norfolk for stealing a petticoat, although there is some doubt as to whether the sentence was carried out. Several children were publicly hanged after the Gordon Riots of 1780.

Perhaps a better indication of when the transition into adulthood started is the age at which a child began work. Records found in urban areas in fourteenth-century France show that apprenticeships were available to those as young as 7, although most boys were in their teens before they signed their contracts. Only half of 16-year-olds were in apprenticeships at that time. Orphaned girls were entitled to contracts and many started before the age of 12. The 1834 Poor Law in England made provision for 'pauper apprentices', who were first placed with craftsmen when they were around 7 or 8.

Following the development of industrialization young people were seen as sources of cheap labour and using them in mines was popular because of their size. Children as young as 8 would not see daylight, spending long periods of time in the darkness of the pit, and working 14-hour days was common. It was not until the mid-nineteenth century – when legislation prohibiting the use of children under 10 in mines was introduced – that the transition from childhood to adulthood moved from about 7 to the early teens (Heywood, 2001). At the beginning of the nineteenth century the mean age for starting work in the mills around Manchester was 11-and-a-half (Heywood, 2001). However, in mills in France and Holland, few girls and no boys younger than 14 were employed.

It is tempting to believe that the age at which young people enter the world of work is somehow fixed, just as children start school at a common age. The evidence shows otherwise. Urban and rural conditions differed. In the nineteenth century, children in rural families would drift into work; they might have performed simple tasks from the age of 7, slowly increasing their commitment until full-time work was finally expected when they entered their teens. The 1851 census reports that only 3.5 per cent of 5- to 9-year-olds were occupied and only 37 per cent of boys and 22 per cent of girls aged 10 to 14 were in 'gainful employment'. Further statistics reveal the type of work undertaken by boys and girls under 15 years of age:

Table 2.1: Main occupations of boys and girls under 15 years of age in Britain in 1851

Boys	000s	%	Girls	000s	%
Agriculture	120	28.4	Textiles	98	41.3
Navigation and docks	82	19.4	Domestic service	71	30.0
			Dress	32	13.5
Mines	37	8.7	Agriculture	17	7.2
Metalwork and tool manufacture	26	6.1	Metalwork and tool manufacture	4	1.7
Dress	23	5.4	Navigation and docks	4	1.7
General labour	15	3.5			
Dealing	12	2.8	Earthenware	3	1.3
Building	11	2.6	Dealing	2	0.8
Domestic service	9	2.1			
Earthenware	6	1.4			

source: Royal Statistical Society, 49 (1886) cited by Heywood, 2001.

In 1843 a Royal Commission on the Employment of Children found that it was commonplace for them to start work in factories from the age of 6 or 7. Their working day was 12 hours, but a 10-year-old could earn almost as much as an adult. Boys regularly entered full-time employment from this age, while girls would learn skills from their mothers and be paid to help in other families. By the age of 12 or 13 they became 'slaveys' employed by wealthier families. In the British census of 1881, nearly half the girls under 15 with an occupation were listed as being in domestic service. In France there are records of girls in their early teens working for up to 16 hours a day.

The economics of using children as sources of income were unavoidable. A weaving family of four in the France of the 1830s would have needed to earn more than 900 francs to pay for basic necessities. With the average wage of only 860 francs, however, new sources of income were needed for clothing and in order to avoid poor diets. Children were good sources and would be used from the age of 7. In England, those whose fathers worked in factories or mines contributed around a quarter of the family's household budget. Charles Booth reported that up to a third of London's working families would be unable to survive on the father's earnings alone, making child labour an essential element of these families' economies.

The introduction of universal education fixed an age at which young people would be expected to become employed. In the late nineteenth century, universal – or near universal – primary education was introduced in England, the United States, and continental Europe. The 1870 Education Act ensured that almost all children attended school at least until the age of 11, while the state assumed responsibilities for defining the minimum duration for education and childhood. This gradually increased for the next 130 years – and looks set to continue following recent political encouragement for young people to participate in some form of education until they are 18.

Extending childhood

The motivations for extending the duration of childhood are debatable. We might see it as charitable that adults wanted to reduce the risk of premature death and increase children's general health and well-being by delaying the age at which they entered employment and were exposed to its inherent dangers. An alternative is the desire to have well-trained and productive workers and fighters who were capable of advancing the ruling classes' economic aspirations. Childhood mortality was much higher among the working classes than among the more professional. An analyst working in early nineteenth-century France estimated that the mean life span for a child born into a professional family was 28; for a child from a tailor's family it was 12, and from a weaver's family only 18 months (Heywood, 2001: 150, though as the author notes the latter figure in particular is 'barely credible'). Another analyst, Flynn, calculated that in the eighteenth and early nineteenth centuries, only half the children born survived past their tenth birthdays. In times when labour was needed for factories or war, it was therefore in a nation's interest to improve the health of its children. A military defeat in Prussia in 1806 spurred interest in using education for national regeneration. Previous attempts at compulsory education can be traced back to seventeenth-century Germany, when legislation in Weimar was introduced. It failed primarily because of a lack of trained teachers, but by the mid-nineteenth century education in Germany was growing, with approximately 80 per cent of children attending school from 6 to 14. Through education people became productive workers and in their enlightenment also reduced crime and disorder.

In the UK successive legislation since 1870 has increased how long young people remain in education:

- the 1870 Education Act made education compulsory from the ages of 5 to 12, although a pupil could leave at the age of 10, if a satisfactory standard had been reached
- the 1918 Fisher Education Act extended the age to 14, eliciting expectation about compulsory part-time education until a person was 18
- the 1944 Education Act raised the school leaving age to 15, advancing speculation about compulsory part-time education until a person was 18
- in 1971 the age was raised to 16. This was effected from 1973
- as of 2013 young people will be expected to participate in education and/or training until they are 17, although current plans do not include penalties for non-participation
- by 2015 participation is expected for 18-year-olds.

For some 16-year-olds who have disengaged, even if they are aware of the increased risks of doing so, raising the age at which they are required to be in education or training might seem unnecessary and even intrusive. Given their alternative set of priorities, extending the age might not be especially welcome.

Rituals and ceremonies

Throughout history formal rituals have denoted the end of childhood. In medieval times young men destined to become knights were apprenticed to older knights who taught courtly and military skills. After a number of years in training the young, would-be knight was 'dubbed' a knight in a formal ceremony that announced the transition was made. Girls from aristocratic families would be similarly schooled by a mistress, whose task was to teach riding, dancing, good manners, and some reading. Such activities were the precursors to marriage and adulthood.

Different faiths mark the transition with various ceremonies such as the Jewish Bar Mitzvah for 13-year-old boys. After the ceremony they have the same rights as an adult and are likewise responsible for their actions. Many lieutenants in seventeenth-century France were only 14, meanwhile, and there is strong evidence of participation in the military of children as young as 11 (Aries, 1960).

We might think of puberty as a transition marked by ritual, however, the age of its onset has changed over time. Better diets, nutrition, and improved general health have lowered the age of puberty from the late to the early teens. Being considered an adult for the purpose of work was not synonymous with the physical changes we now associate with adolescence.

For children from poorer backgrounds, apprenticeships offered predictable career paths. Skills were learned alongside craftsmen through contractual arrangements. Some lasted while others did not. Certain apprenticeships taught children how to read and write. In eighteenth-century Sweden a parish achieved an astonishing literacy rate of more than 90 per cent. Apprenticeships created journeymen and eventually full master craftsmen, whose change in status was marked when they were issued with a certificate in public. The title 'journeyman' probably came from the French *journée* (day), which refers to the entitlement of a day's pay for the work undertaken.

Marriage is marked by public ritual. Chaucer writes of girls marrying at 12 in the fourteenth century, while in the sixteenth Catherine Marion was married at 13 (Aries, 1960). For most of the previous millennium, graduation from school or college was celebrated with a public ceremony.

Formal rituals and routines that mark the transition between childhood or adolescence and adulthood might not be widely recognized today. For some, however, they still exist. Promenade dances (proms) are popular in the UK's secondary schools, giving young people the chance to celebrate leaving the compulsory education system. For those continuing in education, there is the progression from school to college or university and then, hopefully, to a job. Around 80 per cent of university students currently live away from home during term time (BBC, 2009). For many, this marks the start of a gradual process of leaving the family home, one that begins by staying in accommodation provided initially by the college or university and continues, perhaps, by sharing a house with others. At the start of this process students might return to the family home during their vacations. As it progresses, however, many chose to spend more time in their own accommodation and less time in the parental home. The transition from living with a family to living more independently therefore proceeds in stages. If a person has to return to the family home after the end of the course, it can often become problematic for both them and their parents. For the group of young people in the NEET category, such formal transitions are unavailable.

There are other public events, however. Acquiring a driving licence, the ability to vote, receiving a national insurance number, doing jury or military service, having legal access to alcohol in public places, and being subject to adult laws – each of these experiences is age dependent. They indicate a transition, in part, to adulthood.

Modern markers

Postman (1994) has discussed the disappearance of childhood as a separate state. The recognition of childhood as having its own dress code, set of behavioural expectations, skills, and literature is passing. Fashion dictates that, for adults, being attractive means appearing young; children, conversely, aspire to appear older. Just as the development of the printing press created a widespread need for literacy, modern society requires adults to have a similar skill with technology. A generation ago, computer use was restricted to a very small number of people; children show their parents how to work the mobile phone and adolescents teach adults relevant new skills.

Further signs illustrate that the distinction between children and adults is blurring: books, television programmes, and clothes are aimed at both; television advertisements feature adults behaving as children and children behaving as adults; software, both legitimate and viral, can be written by teenagers; computer games are aimed at both groups; public images of children wearing child-specific clothing or styling their hair in ponytails or plaits become steadily less common, yet images of children wearing – and even modelling – adult fashions or hairstyles seem completely normal; many secondary schools have the same uniform for boys and girls – the style is adult and both genders wear long trousers.

Conclusions

This chapter has suggested that the nature, duration, signs, and rituals of childhood have not remained static over time; print, education, and industrial economies have each played their part. Paradoxically, the recent development of mass communication continues to blur the distinction between childhood and adulthood. Our current concern with people who are NEET suggests that our concept of childhood – or perhaps adolescence – has been extended by the state's requirement that young people be involved in educational or other developmental activities at an increasingly older age. We suggest that such an increase is changing how young people interact with systems designed to promote well-being. We no longer think of them as *recipients*, but rather as *consumers* of services. As we extend the influence of educational systems into the lives of young people, we must be careful not to assume that previous habits and customs pertaining to adult/child relationships are still appropriate. History shows us that a 12-year-old's experiences would have varied according to what century they were born in and to which economic class they belonged. So it is with today's teenagers: 17-year-olds are expected to engage with fairly recent cultures that promote training. Understanding how mutable childhood can be might help us clarify two separate approaches towards this new group of young people: those we think ought to be in their best interests and those that actually are. Having considered the changing nature of childhood, we now consider the changing nature of work, training, and education.

Chapter 3

A brief history of employment – the rewards

If childhood, as a concept, has been shaped by history, so too has employment. It is difficult to envisage this phenomenon in any species but mankind; we don't find employers, employees, trade unions, and pension schemes in the animal kingdom, for instance. If we broaden our definition to include differential roles in communities, however, it is not difficult to detect in other mammals evidence of the precursors of employment. Lions, for example, allocate different roles when hunting. Their prey can often run faster than their 50 km/hour. By hunting in packs and encircling the prey they can catch animals capable of running at up to 80 km/hour, a feat only made possible by differentiating certain roles. For the purposes of this study we consider roles that create differences between members of the same gender in the same species. We do not include gender-specific roles that relate purely to reproduction and the rearing of young.

Evolution appears to have enlarged our brains and given us the facility to live in larger communities. When animals live in communities, a degree of role differentiation is valuable. Research looking at the relationship between a species' brain size and how many of that species live together in communities has found that group size is partly determined by habitat; the number of primates in a given social group appears to have an upper limit. Consequentially it has been hypothesized that this limit exists because of cognitive constraints that arise from cortical (brain) size and complexity. Such features affect the number of relationships any individual can sustain (Dunbar, 1993).

Dunbar looked at cortical size and the mean number of social links maintained by individuals for 36 different primate genera. His findings reveal a simple relationship that can be applied to humans to establish how many relationships we can expect to maintain. Dunbar found the number to be about 150. In primate communities the formula is derived from the number of regular grooming partners and the limit to individuals willing to act as allies during conflicts. Time taken for social grooming increases with group size in a virtually linear way. As Dunbar points out, there is a need to balance the distance kept from other group members to protect access to food and safeguard reproductive opportunities with the need not to drive them away completely. An analogue in human terms is the maximum number of people we know well enough to ask a favour from and realistically expect it to be granted (Dunbar, 2003).

While clearly speculative, the theory is gathering credence in a number of different places. Most professional armies have units of about 150; in business, 150 is seen as a critical limit for the effective coordination of tasks through direct person-to-person contact; larger groups need sub-structures that define responsibility and communication (Dunbar, 1993); Kilworth (1984) gave subjects descriptions of 500 different people. The descriptions were realistic but fictional. The subjects were asked if they could identify people they knew who were similar to those described. The mean number was 134 – surprisingly close to the 150 suggested by the cortical-size hypothesis.

In certain communities there is a degree of role differentiation. As Morris (1990) describes, lions live in matriarchies where the senior female – not the male – becomes the dominant leader; baboons have 'oligarchies' in which small groups of males dominate the herd. Younger males are banished until they can steal a female and establish their own oligarchies – which are particularly effective defences against predators since the most powerful in the community cooperate when threatened by an external source that has more power than they have. In a similar way, hierarchical communities establish social dominance through a 'pecking order'. To establish dominance an individual intimidates other community members, who do the same until a hierarchy emerges. The process defines the roles used for feeding and mating; a high-status member of the community gets first access to feeding sites while low-status members are displaced. This type of practice is common among chickens, but present in other species including lemurs, squirrels, and gorillas (Mazur, 1973). Morris (1990), similarly, describes the 'caste system' with insects including termites, ants, bees, and wasps demonstrating role differentiation that he describes as queens, kings, soldiers, and drones. Animal societies organized in such stratified ways offer powerful defences against predators. So role differentiation is not unique to humans but has its roots in our evolutionary history.

It is estimated that of the seven billion humans currently living, around half live in urban environments such as towns and cities. Such demographics imply a high level of sophistication and the need for role differentiation.

Evidence from Stone Age communities suggests some role differentiation in mankind. A site in the English Lake District has revealed a quarry with a small shelter whose stone was used to create axe heads. The distance from the quarry to the comfortable habitats in the area suggests that people engaged in this work and transported the produce to the rest of the community. There is no evidence of the workers' gender or age, but it is likely that they were small in number and worked on behalf of the rest of the community. This is early evidence of employment. The communal efforts required to build Stonehenge, estimated to have begun around 3100 BC, might have involved thirty million hours of labour. Such projects make the rewards of collaboration and cooperation clear: they would not have been possible any other way.

But collaboration need not imply equality. Donkin (2010) reminds us that at some point in history, manual labour became something to get other people to do, if necessary through slavery. In many communities high status implied freedom from manual tasks: if construction tasks could be allocated to the lower classes – allowing those of higher class to avoid the dangers associated with them – so much the better. Similarly, when the day-to-day activities involved in food production could be performed reliably by a workforce of others, this freed the ruling classes for tasks like fighting and reproduction.

Finley has suggested that three conditions are necessary for slavery to develop: the private ownership of land requiring a permanent workforce; the development of commodity production and markets; and the scarcity of alternative internal labour supplies (cited in Donkin, 2010). From the time of written records, slavery has been well documented, occurring in the Greek and Roman eras and throughout nineteenth-century Europe. An early record of slavery in Britain can be found in the Domesday Book of 1087, which showed that slaves were used to provide labour and represented 11 per cent of the population, compared with 71 per cent of landowners. The latter were obliged to provide goods and services to the Manor (Hicks and Allen, 1999), but only around 30 per cent of all produce was traded compared with 90 per cent today. The slaves were a product of international aggression and were not in possession of their own land; survival, therefore, depended on an owner.

While it might obscure important differences, certain parallels arise if we compare the relationship between slave and landowner and that between employee and employer. Certain practices, even today, come uncomfortably close to the slavery of past centuries and bear a striking similarity to those found in oligarchic animal communities.

As the Roman Empire declined, some of its practices survived. The church continued to grow and concentrated its activities in monasteries. Division of labour and role was less in evidence: established members of communities performed the same tasks as their juniors or colleagues who had only recently joined. For those outside the monastery, however, working the land belonging to the church, life was harder. In the twelfth and thirteenth centuries the church managed their estates with the same feudal principles as the landed gentry (Donkin, 2010). The Peasant's Revolt, led by Wat Tyler in 1381, called for the monasteries to have their land removed and given to the people. A modern parallel might be the nationalization of a key industry such as a troubled bank. But for Tyler and his supporters the initiative failed: he was made a victim of a well-planned attack by the established forces loyal to the ruling classes. The peasants were made to continue to work for their lords, masters, and priests, even if the last had taken vows of poverty, while the lords and masters continued to live lives of comparative luxury.

In the mid-fourteenth century the losses to the available workforce caused by the Black Death were particularly influential in big cities such as London, where one estimate put the total number who died at between a third and a half of the population. The reduction increased demands for labour, attracting workers from rural areas into the urban environments searching for better working conditions than those offered by agricultural jobs. As the population left the small communities of rural areas, the stratification created by larger numbers of people living together became apparent.

With the mechanization of cloth production using water-powered mills, industry also grew. Those with the economic power to build the plant benefited from economies of scale. A water-powered roller was quicker and more efficient at kneading cloth than conventional human muscles. The harnessing of energy and the development of technology to manufacture essentials set the agenda for the next six hundred years. The distinction between employer and employee was cast.

Technology began to drive change. The invention of mass-produced print in the mid-fifteenth century not only created a new industry but a much more efficient way of transmitting information. Ideas that advanced the well-being of those who could promote them quickly spread across Europe. As religion remained at the core of these ideas, and with it the desirability of work, the work ethic was being enshrined in religious thought, particularly north of the Alps.

Martin Luther's challenge to the conventional Catholic Church contained a view that the Church had become corrupt. Believing that salvation came through faith rather than payment, Luther protested against the widespread practice of selling indulgences to the wealthy so that their sins might be forgiven. The Pope excommunicated him in 1521. Luther was active in the German Peasants' War of 1524 and went on to publish a German translation of the Bible in 1534. The teachings in the Bible of hard work and abstinence became the foundations of the Protestant work ethic that still resonates today. Our concerns about people in the NEET category come, in some part, from a view that work is good and we ought to engage in it.

Following such developments, Puritanism emerged. In Scotland, Calvin's ideas found favour with John Knox, pilgrims sailed to the New World to create a better land, and the English monasteries were dissolved by a powerful king whose life and loves were disapproved of by the Pope. King Henry VIII's motives might have been self-serving but the split with Rome had far-reaching consequences, particularly for the employer who could now appeal to the new religious work ethic as a motivational tool. If God had worked hard to create Heaven and Earth, then man must surely work hard to follow the path to paradise. In 1648 idleness was made illegal in Massachusetts (Donkin, 2010), while Bunyan's *The Pilgrim's Progress*, published in 1678, extolled the virtues of 'the straight and narrow way'. The book sold 100,000 copies in England during his lifetime and was reprinted in America three years later. Work was synonymous with the purity of life, avoidance of temptation, and the freedom from sin required for salvation.

Followers of this philosophy were not always popular. The Quakers of the mid-seventeenth century wore plain clothes, refused to pay tithes to the church, or swear oaths in court and accordingly became unemployable in certain professions such as the law. However, their principles resulted in some spectacular commercial successes: they founded brand names, for instance – Barclays, Cadbury, and Rowntree among them – that are still used today. Later, their commitment to work and their employees led to the building of whole communities comprising housing, schools, and leisure facilities; the Bourneville community in Birmingham is one example. Each of these developments increased the importance of work, which continued to be organized by an employer and carried out by an employee.

It is the Industrial Revolution, however, that is most often credited as the origin of modern employment practices. The discovery of large-scale industrial processes, able to supply new materials and items previously only available to the wealthy, significantly changed how work was organized.

Defining the origins of the Industrial Revolution is more difficult than documenting its influence. Donkin (2010) attributes it to the development of iron foundries in Ironbridge by Abraham Darby in 1709; Galbi (1994) suggests that it was the large-scale cotton mills that grew slightly later. Whichever view we take, however, there is no doubt that economies of scale, facilitated by large machinery or processes requiring many operators, significantly impelled the separation of tasks and the specialization of workers in the iron foundries. The possibility of mass producing a better iron cooking pot drove development and the subsequent profits. The earlier creation of yarn by home workers needed no more than three people to operate the wheel; at Cromford, the water mill powering the spinning frame employed 300, a number that rose to 800 by 1789. Such development firmly established the distinction between employer and employee.

Other influences played their part. The new mass transport service provided by the steam train enabled workers to travel more easily. Many labourers travelled in search of better lives. The exodus of Irish families after the potato famine of 1847 created a large population of unskilled workers. Lists of passengers who arrived in New York between 1836 and 1853 revealed that fewer than 5 per cent had previous industrial experience. If you arrive in a new country with little money, farming will not be easy, whereas a position in a large factory might be more accessible. Prior to the famine most of the immigrants to the United States were skilled and relatively wealthy (Sukkoo, 2007). Employees could receive payment reasonably quickly, albeit at a low level.

The work practices familiar today soon evolved. Clocking on was introduced in the early 1800s and work was standardized so different workers could undertake the same function if a particular individual was unable or unwilling to do so. There were difficulties. Increased mechanization reduced the number of workers required to produce the same output. In France, an inventor was mobbed and almost drowned in 1804 when he demonstrated an improved loom. In 1812 Ned Ludd inspired a movement to destroy the new equipment that threatened work. Luddites smashed machinery and set fire to mills in an attempt to stop the reduction of work and pay at a time of rising food prices.

But technology is hard to fight. It produced more efficient methods of transport and production following vast investment in the eighteenth century. As a network of inland waterways linking rivers and cities developed it was possible to transport heavy produce from Liverpool to Hull by boat. A horse and cart could carry about 2 tonnes by road but the same horse could pull 40 tonnes by water. At the time this was considered revolutionary: an ingenious project in which to invest. No investor could have foreseen the arrival of the railway and the consequent loss of utility to the waterways.

Institutions developed to assist the individual worker's rights. As machines became increasingly efficient, fewer workers were required. Pay was determined by the employer and wages dropped. In 1834, Robert Owen set up the 'Grand National Consolidated Trades Union'. Six workers in Tolpuddle, a village in Dorset, tried to form a similar organization using the Friendly Society framework. Employers regarded the action as a threat and secured convictions (on the obscure ground of 'administering oaths' of membership, since membership itself was no longer illegal) that led to punishment by transportation for seven years. The Trade Union movement soon grew, attracting 10,000 people to its meetings. Later, when that number reached 30,000, the force of its ideas was recognized by the government and the 'Tolpuddle martyrs' had their sentences reduced, though not repealed.

The economics of being an employer – as opposed to an employee – were staggering. Many at the bottom end of the social scale had to supplement their income by prostitution, while employers at the top enjoyed the type of riches previously only available to the landed gentry. Benjamin Gott, a Leeds mill owner, filled his manor house with art works from Europe's finest and most expensive artists: among them were Titian, Canaletto, Caravaggio, and Brueghel. In 2011 a single Titian masterpiece attracted $16.8 million at auction in New York.

For many in the nineteenth century there were alternatives to employment. Coinciding with the development of the professional, in 1800 surgeons came together to form the Royal College of Surgeons, lawyers formed The Law Society in 1825 and architects created the Royal Institute of British Architects in 1834. There are many such examples. Professionals offered their services without the need for employers, but they were few in number compared with manual labourers.

As the century progressed, the relationship between employee and employer strengthened and the concept and benefits of a production line were clarified. Henry Ford is regarded as having understood this well and the ability to move the goods instead of the workers led to huge reductions in manufacturing costs for individual items. Donkin (2010) reminds us that the famous Model T Ford cost $950 in 1909 but only $360 in 1916. The huge savings resulted purely from the efficiency of the production line that was superior to static alternatives, but there was a human cost. Such was the production line's unpopularity that workforce turnover rose from 380 per cent early in 1913 to 900 per cent in later years. Only readily available immigrant workers enabled the factory to continue. However, the huge profits generated by the industry allowed the company to raise the daily rate for production line workers to nearly 50 per cent higher than that paid in other industries. Workers stayed and wages rose by nearly 50 per cent between 1870 and 1913 (O'Rourke and Williamson, 1999). It paid to be an employee, even if the work was repetitive and boring.

In an attempt to understand the increasing efficiency, a factory in Chicago became the centre of a series of experiments that led its owner to give his name to one of the more celebrated concepts in psychology. The factory was Hawthorne Works, run by General Electric. The owners changed how much light was used in the factory to illuminate the production line. They hoped to discover what specific quantity was optimal for production and efficiency. While the motivation was undoubtedly to maximize efficiency of production, as the factory also made electric lighting they wished to increase sales as a result. Though the findings of the study were never published – they showed that production increased whether the lighting got brighter or dimmer and were therefore unlikely to increase sales – this became known as the 'Hawthorne Effect' representing the willingness of employers to study manufacturing practices and the impact they have on output.

The twentieth century advanced thinking about employment. As records from 1909 indicate, the terms 'career', 'vocation' and 'occupation' had been used more or less interchangeably (Parsons 1909 cited in Patton and McMahon, 2001). As the status of employees and employment grew, however, theories developed by universities suggested that the course of a person's life could be tracked and described in terms of the work they did. As Hicks and Allen (1999) demonstrate, professional and managerial work increased in popularity as people moved away from work that was unskilled to partly skilled:

Table 3.1: Distribution of professional groups, 1911 and 1991

		1911 (%)	1991 (%)
I	Professional	1	5
II	Managerial and technical	13	32
III	Skilled	37	34
IV	Partly skilled	39	22
V	Unskilled	10	6

By the 1950s theories outlining career stages as development paths were published. Donald Super, the most cited author, produced a wide range of papers describing his theory of vocational choice between 1939 and 1990. Super (1954) set out a six-stage model:

- the crystallization stage (age 14–18)
- the specification stage (age 18–21)
- the implementation stage (age 21–24)
- the stabilization stage (age 24–35)
- the consolidation stage (age 35)
- readiness for retirement (age 55).

Super's model suggests an identifiable path along which employees travel. It also assumes that an individual has a high degree of personal choice. Though it recognizes the variety of roles that people occupy – work, home, friends, etc. – with the absence of references to unemployment, redundancy, and economic conditions, most pertinent is the centrality of work. Writers such as Charles Handy later questioned our dependence on large organizations to arrange our work. He even suggested that single careers or skill sets were not appropriate since a person might not work in the same sector – let alone the same organization – for their entire lives. Handy proposed a 'portfolio' of skills, roles, and functions that would enable an individual to offer different services to different organizations, some paid and others not. He highlighted the benefits of small-scale operations and groups of individuals offering similar services, much like the co-operative model. Other writers were also suggesting that organizations had grown too big and needed to have flatter management structures (Peters, 1985).

When we consider our concern about young people who are NEET, it might be necessary to broaden our definitions of work and training to include roles that could traditionally have been excluded. Consider the role of eBay as providing a trading opportunity, for example. Though small in scale it can offer marketing prospects to a vast range of potential consumers. The assumptions that fashioned the distinction between employer and employee in the late seventeenth and early eighteenth centuries might no longer apply. Today, successful trade might not require large equipment or plant; it might not require large numbers of staff to be managed centrally; and it might no longer require employment according to the sense that has evolved over the last four centuries.

For a 16-year-old coming to the end of compulsory education, many options are available. However, in most previous generations finding work was easy; today things are harder and opportunities more limited.

Following the political aspiration to raise the participation age to 18, young people are being encouraged to stay on in full-time education or training for longer. For some this might involve going into a sixth form or college, continuing to study chosen subjects that could lead to university or undertaking vocational studies that might lead them into a profession. Different educational environments offer viable alternatives for young people. In an urban area with an annual cohort of 3,500 students, 84 per cent chose this option in 2011. Of that group, 36 per cent chose to remain at school.

A sixth form is an extension of school, whose environment is often smaller. The facilities and range of subjects available can vary significantly. The sixth form offers young people the following advantages: of studying more than one subject and gaining different types of qualification; if they choose to stay on at their own sixth form, familiarity with the environment and teachers – often cited as attractions when making this particular decision; and the structured learning process that provides them with greater confidence to do well and is often the style that more of them prefer. A person considering this option needs to take into account whether they enjoyed school up to 16 and if the subjects they would like to study are offered.

For those who want to stay in full-time education but feel as though they require a change, colleges present an alternative option, one taken by 48 per cent of the 2011 cohort. The learning structure is different in colleges as they often offer a greater number of vocational qualifications. The environment is also bigger and focuses on motivation. Students are expected to become independent learners. Many young people like the challenge of a new environment and while some might be anxious about meeting new people, this is often overcome.

Differences in structure give young people options and, until recently, financial support for travel and study expenses while in full-time study or training. The means-tested Educational Maintenance Allowance (EMA) meant many young people received money while they continued studying. Since its removal, however, students have to consider financial implications, with many forced to look for part-time employment that will fit around their studies. While some support might be available, it varies according to each institution.

For students wanting to continue in education who either cannot cope full-time or wish to build on existing skills, a further option is a foundation learning programme delivered through a local training provider. These focus on developing proficiency in English, maths, and information and communication technology (ICT), alongside employability skills. Such provision often enhances a person's job prospects and will ideally be tailored to them and their needs. As well as focusing on employability skills, it provides opportunities to go on work placements where they can gain experience. Students respond well to these programmes in the following two scenarios: if they have struggled with the intensity of school or if they are not yet job-ready. To combat any financial issues this group of young people faces, many training providers help with travel expenses and have bonus schemes dependent on attendance and meeting personal targets. Of the cited cohort, 6.1 per cent chose this option.

Other people prefer to leave the education system at 16 to enter paid employment. While many will lack training, working in a company as a full-time employee provides a chance to move up and gain transferable skills.

A further option is apprenticeship, which gives people a training wage and time off to study to complete a work-based qualification. While extremely popular, opportunities are limited. The competition for such vacancies is high and young people often offer skills they have already gained from hobbies in addition to those learned at school. To be successful they require a level of proficiency in English and maths and they must be prepared for the world of work. Many require previous experience to confirm their employability, which is often hard for them to build up. Only 0.44 per cent of our cohort was accepted onto an apprenticeship, 0.74 per cent commenced a job with training, and 0.68 per cent a job without training.

A small number (0.5 per cent) engaged in part-time learning, part-time employment, or voluntary and personal development activities.

Those young people who are not prepared to continue with any type of further education or training but are unable to gain a paid position end up being classed as NEET. While some go into voluntary positions to gain work experience, others have personal circumstances that prevent them from making positive choices. Such individuals accounted for 4.3 per cent of the cohort in 2011.

Let us consider the available options when leaving statutory education and the decisions made by four individuals who are currently 16.

Joseph

Joseph was looking to go to university in the future. To do this, he was going to continue with full-time education after Year 11. When it came to making the decision Joseph had several things to consider. First, what courses would help him get to university. He wanted to become a sports teacher and knew he would need to continue with his sport. However, sport could be studied in different ways, at different levels, and at a number of institutions. Joseph considered his own learning style and the fact that he wanted to keep his options open by taking other subjects. After a lot of thought, he chose the structure of a sixth form environment and found one that offered the type of course he wanted as well as the other subjects he was interested in. Joseph has settled in well and feels he made the right choice.

Ayesha

Ayesha chose to do a student apprenticeship throughout school, alongside her core curriculum subjects. It gave her an insight into work-based learning that she enjoyed. At the end of Year 11, Ayesha wanted to move into an apprenticeship. As EMA had ceased, she wanted to earn money after leaving school and knew that would be impossible if she went to college full-time, unless she got a part-time job. She also preferred the practical way of learning.

Ayesha started looking for a childcare apprenticeship but her search proved very difficult and she was unsuccessful for most of the year. She decided she would apply for a full-time course as a back-up, as this would involve some practical work, if not a paid wage. Fortunately, when Ayesha left in June, she secured a childcare apprenticeship through a local training provider. She is now studying for a National Vocational Qualification (NVQ) while working in a local nursery, where she receives a training wage.

Claire

Throughout Year 11, Claire struggled with her post-16 options. She had very little confidence and despite wanting to continue with her studies, was very nervous about college or sixth form and what subjects to choose. Claire was expected to achieve low grades and had learning difficulties that contributed to her anxiety. Her friends were all going to a local college and she gave in to peer pressure and applied. Claire was too nervous to go to the interview but with the school's support she started looking at other options. She found a smaller training programme that could increase her basic skills and confidence and perhaps be a stepping stone towards going to college. The training programme also offered work tasters to uncover what Claire might like to do in the future. Claire is now doing well and is aiming to go to college this year.

In each of these cases another outcome was possible: entering the NEET category. Those in this cohort, however, tend to have complex and unstable lives. The sources of that instability might be varied, but the greater it is, the more likely the person will not engage in education, employment, or training. The next case study starts to illustrate these points.

Anthony

Anthony had been on alternative provision throughout most of Year 11 as he didn't engage at school. When considering his post-16 options, he wanted to do something practical. His main interest was construction. Anthony wanted an apprenticeship to start earning money and would not consider learning in any other form. Unfortunately, construction is a very competitive industry and opportunities are limited. At this time, Anthony's mother became very ill. His attendance became sporadic in consequence and his need for financial help increased. With very limited basic skills and a high level of absence, Anthony did not gain the entry requirements for many opportunities. He was unsuccessful in finding an apprenticeship and was unwilling to start a training programme that offered him no financial gain. Anthony ended up NEET and now looks after his mother.

Conclusion

Having examined the history of employment we suggest that the employee/employer relationship that has developed over the last millennium might not be the only model for economic activity in the future. Understanding how both parties and their relationship evolved might free us from assumptions that perhaps are no longer useful. As Anthony's case highlights, while activity within the family might not be recognized as education, employment, or training, it can still offer a positive and meaningful role for all concerned. The circumstances in which young people enter the NEET category often arise from complex and sometimes chaotic social conditions. Understanding these conditions permits us to see those involved in new ways and suggest alternative approaches to enhance life chances.

Chapter 4

Developing a local screening tool

Screening populations

Screening is found in a wide range of settings, from healthcare and education to road traffic accident reduction and airport security. Successful applications of screening programmes have a number of prerequisites:

There exist measurable factors associated with the outcome being screened for. In a health screen, for example, the risk of contracting a particular disease is determined by looking at factors such as aspects of lifestyle or existing biological features. These factors should be distinct from those occurring at random or as a result of relationships that are too complex to predict. It is essential to understand the difference between causality and association. Poverty, for instance, is known to be linked to lower life expectancy (Wagstaff, 2002), but it is not a person's bank balance that is directly responsible for early death, rather the implications of there being fewer funds available to spend on the components of a healthy lifestyle including good nutrition and exercise.

Factors are sufficiently discrete to effectively discriminate between those individuals (or groups) who are at risk and those who are not. Marginal differences between groups may be statistically significant when large populations are examined, but with so many exceptions, applying the information would lead to too many errors. Consider the following ideal situation in which a risk factor is present in half of the population:

Table 4.1: Hypothetical distribution of risk factors and outcomes

Risk factor	Outcome
Present 50%	50% Negative 0% Positive
Absent 50%	50% Positive 0% Negative

While such certainty reflects a correlation of 1, these correlations are not found in real populations. The following figures are hypothetical but represent real situations with greater accuracy:

Table 4.2: Hypothetical distribution of risk factors and outcomes

Risk factor	Outcome
Present 50%	30% Negative 20% Positive
Absent 50%	15% Positive 35% Negative

If interventions were based purely on the presence of the risk factor, 20 per cent of the population would needlessly have been subject to the additional service while a further 15 per cent who actually needed it would not receive it. While the screen might be said to be successful 65 per cent of the time, an error rate of one in two might be unacceptable, particularly if an intervention has any negative implications.

Factors must be robust over time. While that might seem obvious, it is not always the case. An individual involved in a traffic accident might have run across the road without looking for oncoming traffic; they might have seen a bus arriving that they needed to catch. The accident might have happened because the person was late for an appointment and needed to be on the bus, but such a factor is almost certainly transient. By contrast, health outcomes can be influenced by behavioural features such as smoking. If smoking is a long-term habit it could form part of a health screening tool.

It is economically viable and socially acceptable to collect data about the factors for a population. If the data are simply too expensive to collect, there is no rationale for conducting the screen. While a great deal of information could be collected about an individual, the cost of the exercise could exceed any possible benefits. A similar factor to consider is the consent of the population. Many civil liberty groups question and resist the state's attempts to collect large amounts of information about individuals.

There are certain interventions that, if executed early, promote better outcomes for the individuals affected than if they are not utilized or are utilized later. Early intervention is often very favourable, especially for those reacting to difficult situations. However, the need for early intervention is often difficult to recognize if there are no external signs that it is necessary. This can lead to potentially affected parties having difficulties engaging.

There is a political aspiration, reflecting public opinion, that such exercises are legitimate ways of promoting the population's best interests.

The potential benefits, however, are varied and widespread.

Early intervention

If there is anything to be gained from early intervention, screening will be necessary to identify those who require it. A number of problems would be addressed more comprehensively if they were caught before extensive damage occurred. For motor accident prevention, cars were more likely to be involved in breakdowns and accidents if they had not been maintained well. Introducing a compulsory screening inspection for all vehicles over three years old (the MOT test) intended to reduce the number of unroadworthy cars and reduce the expenditure on expensive accident damage by ensuring that the major controls (such as brakes and steering) are in good working order.

Targeting of resources

If interventions are expensive, screening can identify those who will potentially benefit the most. It also provides both a model and rationale for not intervening with other low-risk groups or individuals. Some services currently offered to all people may be just as effective if targeted at the most vulnerable because the least vulnerable do not benefit from the service; targeting can therefore reduce costs. To refer back to the previous example, the MOT inspection is not universal but it is targeted at cars that are no longer new.

Evaluation of intervention

Traditional methods of evaluating projects use methodologies whose roots are empiricist. The gold standard often held up for such research is the randomized clinical trial (RCT). At least two groups are identified and membership of each is randomized. An intervention is undertaken with one group but not with the other. Where possible, the intervention and data collection should be conducted by parties who know no more than is necessary to administer the tests. The data processing reveals any differences between the groups that are attributed to the intervention.

However, there can be ethical difficulties in assigning individuals to the intervention or experimental group. Pawson and Tilley (1997) describe the challenges facing social scientists when they try to apply randomized clinical trial (RCT) studies. Using a screening tool can identify groups with similarities and predicted outcomes, allowing an innovation to be undertaken without the need for a control group. Outcomes for the experimental group can be compared with those with similar profiles, and may likewise be attributed to the intervention. Though it is necessary to accept the compromises that come when using this method, it avoids the ethical issues associated with selection.

When the MOT test was introduced, it did not use an RCT evaluation method. The reduction in the number of car breakdowns and accidents was attributed to the screening provided by the MOT test.

There are additional hazards. A link has been found between one factor and an outcome. It may be described as *highly statistically significant*, which is often misinterpreted as *highly significant*. To illustrate this, we refer to the discovery about a link between Attention Deficit Hyperactive Disorder (ADHD) and the presence of a rare variation in the person's DNA. This hypothesis was reported widely in September 2010 and led to public discussions of the genetic cause of ADHD and the possible introduction of screening. The details are worth examining.

There are three elements to this research:

- the incidence of ADHD is around 5 per cent of a school population
- the DNA variation is present in 14 per cent of children with ADHD
- the same DNA variation is present in only 7 per cent of the rest of the population.

Reports that the differences are statistically significant are correct, but let us look at what happens when you apply the statistics to the population of a school.

Consider a school of 1,000 students:

- 5 per cent may have ADHD – or 50 students
- 95 per cent will not have ADHD – or 950 students
- of those students with ADHD, 14 per cent will have the genetic variation – 7 students
- of those students with ADHD, 86 per cent will not have the genetic variation – 43 students
- of those students without ADHD, 7 per cent will have the genetic variation – 66.5 students
- of those students without ADHD, 93 per cent will not have the genetic variation – 883.5 students.

We can express this in a table:

Table 4.3: Correlation of ADHD and genetic variation

School with 1,000 students	With ADHD	Without ADHD
With genetic variation	7	66.5
Without genetic variation	43	883.5

While presenting slightly artificial numbers is less than ideal – we cannot logically have half a student – the point is clear. The genetic screen would identify 7 students, miss 66.5 students, and wrongly attribute the risk of ADHD to a further 43. In other words, it would get it wrong for 109.5 students and right for just 7.5. Clearly, screening would be inadvisable in such circumstances.

We offer this example to illustrate the distinction between risk factors that are statistically significant but have low predictability and risk factors that are statistically significant and have high predictability.

Screening in education

The mass testing or screening of populations of children is not new. While standardized assessment tasks (SATs) are comparatively recent developments, they are part of a tradition that has a long, if controversial, history. Screening is not value free and in many ways reflects the political thinking of the time. But values can change over time. Consider the following example:

When the 1944 Education Act raised the age of compulsory education to 14, the 11-plus examination was introduced at the same time. It was used to select or segregate pupils according to scores on tests of intelligence. Those with high scores went to grammar schools; the others to secondary moderns. The examination was built on ideas developed in the 1920s described in a government-commissioned report that used research from the previous century. In it the author shows he is aware that intelligence tests were viewed with suspicion because they were assumed to be foreign. Referring to the concept of a mental test, the author refutes this criticism:

> The conception of the mental test, to whatever extent it may have been developed and applied in recent years in other countries, was originally put forward by an English scientist. It was Sir Francis Galton who, in 1883, first announced the possibility of measuring intellectual abilities by simple laboratory tests. Galton's interest, however, was subsequently diverted towards problems of anthropology and eugenics.
>
> (Selbye Bigge, 1924: 5)

Using a mental test was consequently promoted and one benefit of adopting screening in education was its potential to improve mankind by selective breeding, if necessary, of races of humans chosen for their intelligence. A major contributor to the 1924 report was the first educational psychologist, Cyril Burt. In Burt's book *The Young Delinquent* he considers at some length the eugenic solutions to delinquency:

They [eugenic solutions] would, of necessity, be based primarily upon eugenic principles – to segregate or sterilize all who openly manifest, or carry in latent form, the seeds of a criminal disposition, until at last the breed becomes extinct.

(Burt, 1927: 5)

Such a chilling idea predated the slaughtering of Jews in the decade following – which emphasizes that the purposes of screening must always be clear and ethical.

Burt, in fact, rejected the ideas, noting the necessity of proving that criminality was inherited. He wrote:

What are the signs and symptoms by which its [criminal] presence might be recognized beyond the chance of a mistake. Such proofs and such discoveries have never yet been made.

(ibid.: 59)

Subsequent dissatisfaction with intelligence testing and segregation saw it removed as a tool for school selection at the point of transition from primary to secondary. This type of screening did not have the support of the people, nor was it well regarded in contemporary thinking.

However, there are benefits to screening in child development and education: prenatal checks are available for a range of disabling conditions; post-natal checks for development in the first two years of life aim to identify children with developmental difficulties; and profiles of pupils' development are drafted between nursery and school and can be used to identify those who require differentiated programmes of study. At the time of writing the Department for Education has just announced a screening programme for reading prior to 10-year-olds transferring to secondary school.

Note: there is now a trend for academies to set entrance examinations, a practice that comes close to screening populations for school selection. The arguments for this practice relate to raising educational standards.

Screening and NEET

Screening for young people at risk of entering the NEET category must satisfy the same criteria we have outlined above, and additionally consider the issue of different regional characteristics.

The incidence of young people in the NEET category varies widely throughout the UK. In 2007 the lowest and highest incidences were in Torquay and Norfolk respectively, standing at less than 1 per cent in the former region and more than 20 per cent in the latter. Though the term NEET has been applied to both areas, it is possible, even likely, that the groups have quite different characteristics.

A study dating back to 1995 illustrates this hypothesis. Examining the factors associated with non-attendance at school, Arnold *et al.* (1995) looked at two neighbouring secondary schools in a borough of the West Midlands. After collecting data on 13 possible risk factors, two stood out that surprised the authors: first, out of the 13 possible risk factors, most were not associated with poor attendance and just three were able to model most of the attendance that was attributable to the researched items, and second, these three were different between the two schools. Though two of the factors were the same, the third was different. After further investigation it emerged that teenage girls in one area were under pressure to look after their grandparents, unlike those from families in the other catchment area. This resulted in lower attendance rates among girls than boys. The screening tools that were used differed between the two schools, but both significantly reduced the rate of truancy through early intervention.

Studies like these suggest a rationale for developing local screening tools to identify local factors that might be complex and subject to local variation. While not the only approach, it is increasingly being used in this way in areas including Wakefield, Coventry, and Ealing.

The method we have adopted has a sequence of stages:

- list all possible contextual risk factors
- consider the economics of data collection
- decide the feasibility of data collection
- decide on the sampling method (possibly use a pilot)
- collect data
- analyse data – build model
- test model in a school (Year 8 or 9)
- build interventions
- evaluate.

Practical example

Stage one: list all possible contextual risk factors

A group of professionals from the Connexions service was invited to collaborate with local psychologists. They were asked to list any factor that they considered relevant to becoming NEET. The group was reassured that no contribution, however unusual, would be unwelcome. The list was as follows:

Home issues – poor parental capacity

Low basic skills

Disability

History of exclusion

Poor behaviour

Homelessness

Drug and substance abuse

Poor social skills

History of offending

Gender

Undiagnosed dyslexia

Poor school attendance

Poor attitude

Looked-after children

Not prepared to travel

Travelling children

History of abuse

Teenage parent

Low motivation/aspiration

'Just want a job'

Mental health issues

Young carer

Unemployment in family

Ethnic origin

Single parent

Stage two: consider the economics of data collection

The group examined the data that was central and inexpensive to access. It was differentiated from data that would require additional, and probably expensive, research. Central data was coded 1 and additional data 2. The list became:

Home issues – poor parental capacity 1

Low basic skills 1

Disability 1

History of exclusion 1

Poor behaviour 1

Homelessness 2

Drug and substance abuse 2

Poor social skills 2

History of offending 1

Gender 1

Undiagnosed dyslexia 1

Poor school attendance 1

Poor attitude 2

Looked-after children 1

Not prepared to travel 2

Travelling children 1

History of abuse 2

Teenage parent 1

Low motivation/aspiration 2

'Just want a job' 2

Mental health issues 2

Young carer 1

Unemployment in family 2

Ethnic origin 1

Single parent 2

Some work additionally took place to operationalize the categories. The 'history of offending' category was changed to 'known to the youth offending team (YOT)'. The 'low motivation/aspiration' category was defined as pupils' response to a simple question: 'what do you want to do when you leave school?'. If the answer indicated something specific, the person would be categorized as having a degree of aspiration and motivation. If their response was something like 'don't know' or 'stay home', however, the person was placed in the 'low motivation/aspiration' category. The 'drug and substance abuse' category was defined as 'known to the drug education team' (DECCA) while young people who had moved accommodation within the previous year were considered as having 'accommodation issues'.

Stage three: decide the feasibility of data collection

This stage involved a practical examination of how much additional data could be collected for large groups of children. A number of data items were considered too difficult or expensive to collect, leading us to discount a number of factors that could in other circumstances justifiably be considered. The list shortened to:

Accommodation issues	Gender
Low motivation	Ethnicity
Behaviour issues	Young carer
Unemployment in family	Known to DECCA (drug team)
Poor basic skills	Not prepared to travel
Known to YOT	Single parent
School attendance < 80 per cent	Travelling person
LDD	Looked-after children

Stage four: decide on the sampling method

The questions we addressed are those cited at the beginning of this chapter. It was essential to establish if there were significant differences between the target group (NEET) and others who are not in this group (EET). The number of factors investigated in this study reflected the time available to the research team. Different studies vary widely in the amount of data.

A sample was taken of 40 17-year-olds who are currently in the NEET category. It was balanced against a group of 39 others, of whom 13 were in education, 13 in employment and the remaining 13 in training. The sampling method enabled comparisons between the following groups: NEET v EET; Employed v NEET; Education v NEET; and Training v NEET.

Stage five: data collection

A total of 79 17-year-olds were sampled. Data was collected from existing sources and databases, but each person was interviewed using the same questions. Some interviews took place over the telephone and some occurred in person. All the data was collected anonymously and collated on a simple spreadsheet.

Stage six: analyse data and build model

The data was arranged in a simple 1 = present and 0 = absent matrix. Analyses were targeted at significant differences between the NEET and the EET groups, while additional differences – between the NEET and Education, NEET and Employment and NEET and Training groups – were also examined. All the analyses used SPSS (PC) v14.

Significant differences were found across the following categories:

Table 4.4: Relative significance of relevant issues

Significant	Not significant
Accommodation issues	Gender
Low motivation	Ethnicity
Behaviour issues	Young carer
Unemployment in family	Known to DECCA
Poor basic skills	Not prepared to travel
Known to YOT	Single parent
School attendance < 80 per cent	Travelling person
LDD	Looked-after children

Further analysis revealed those factors that were consistent across two or three comparisons. Comparing the NEET group with those in education, employment, and training respectively, for example, highlighted significant differences with regard to accommodation issues. Other factors were only significant for one or two comparisons. If a factor significantly differed in all three categories, it was weighted as 3; if it appeared in two out of three groups, it was weighted as 2; and if it appeared in only one comparison, it was weighted as 1. The weighted factors were as follows:

Table 4.5: Weighting of factors

Factor	Weighting
Accommodation issues	3
Low motivation	3
Behaviour issues	2
Unemployment in family	2
Poor basic skills	2
Known to YOT	1
School attendance < 80 per cent	1
LDD	1

A number of statistical techniques will produce better weightings and are used by the Audit Commission report (2010) because of their greater sophistication. This method, however, is relatively easy to use and can be explained to different stakeholders without much confusion. It can also be used with relatively small numbers such as those in the pilot.

We had built up the model using a simple spreadsheet. Zero was used if the factor was absent and 1 was used if it was present. The model generated in the pilot in Westbury was:

Weighted risk factor score = (3x accommodation issues) + (3x low motivation) + (2x behaviour issues) + (2x unemployment in family) + (2x poor basic skills) + (known to YOT) + (school attendance < 80%) + (LDD)

The maximum score is 15.

Stage seven: test model in a school

A secondary school agreed to act as the pilot for a whole-year-group screen. Personal advisers from Connexions collected data on 181 pupils in Year 9. The data produced the following results:

Out of a year group of 181: (n=181)

108 had 0
16 had 1
13 had 2
14 had 3
8 had 4
6 had 5
3 had 6
2 had 7
5 had 8
3 had 10
2 had 12
1 had 14

Expressed as a graph the results looked like this:

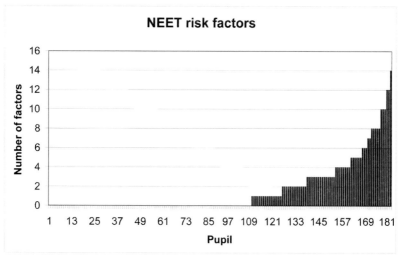

Figure 4.1: Number of risk factors in pilot school

The shape of the graph's curve is essentially Poissonian, which reflects the high incidence of very low (or no) risk factors and higher numbers of risk factors for successively smaller numbers of pupils.

Stage eight: build interventions

Four groups of people emerged from the data. These groups were created quite pragmatically. Each group had a different type of intervention, with the high-risk group given the highest number of additional services.

The categories and interventions were as follows:

10–14 score (n=6): Personal contact with young person and/or family. Tracking throughout Year 10/11. Enrichment activities focusing on post-16 options

6–9 score (n=10): Initial contact by phone or in school – tracked though BTEC in vocational studies group

1–5 score (n=57): Nothing additional

0 (n=108): Nothing additional.

Stage nine: evaluation

The nature of the project did not lend itself to randomized clinical trials, as that would have required each group to be split into two with interventions undertaken with only one. Practically this was not possible within this context.

The outcomes from this project can be seen when presented in the following table:

Table 4.6: Outcome matrix

Factor	Outcome NEET	Outcome EET
Risk factors present	(A)	(C)
Risk factors absent	(B)	(D)

With the first cohort, however, interventions were undertaken in the 'risk factors present' group, which compromised the fidelity of cells A and C. If the interventions were successful we would expect cell A to be 0 or close to 0 and cell C to represent those with identified risk factors. Cell B is important to consider. These are those pupils who were not identified as being at risk of becoming NEET and consequently did not receive any additional preventative interventions.

By looking at the results, however, it is possible to indicate some of the benefits the screening and interventions provided.

Results for the different groups were subject to a range of analytical tools. Individuals in each risk category were divided into 'easy' or 'hard to work with'. The raw data looks like this:

Table 4.7: Results

	No risk (108)	Low risk (55)	Medium risk (10)	High risk (6)
Enhanced involvement	2	11	10	6
Standard involvement	106	44	0	0

If we aggregate the 'no' and 'low risk' together and aggregate the 'medium' and 'high risk', this becomes:

Table 4.8: Involvement and risk groups

	Enhanced involvement	Standard involvement
Medium/high risk	16	0
No/low risk	13	150

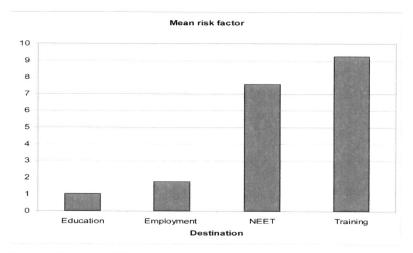

Figure 4.2: Mean risk factor scores by destination groups

Figure 4.2 highlights significant differences between the following individuals: those who are NEET or in training and those who are in education or employment. There were no significant differences between those in education or employment or between those who were NEET or in training.

Furthermore, young people entering employment directly from school are not from higher risk groups than others, particularly the vast majority who stay on in education.

The similarity in the profiles of those in NEET and training groups reflects the work that Connexions personal advisers do with especially vulnerable young people. For those who might become NEET after leaving school, being allocated a training place is easier than obtaining employment – while continuing with education will only be possible if they can be shown the benefits of doing so.

The first cohort our study screened left school in the summer of 2010. The screen took place at the end of Year 8 and beginning of Year 9. The information was used to allocate a small additional resource to students: those in the highest risk group received home visits and were monitored closely every month, while those in the medium risk group were encouraged to undertake the BTEC in vocational studies.

The outcomes are shown in figure 4.3 below:

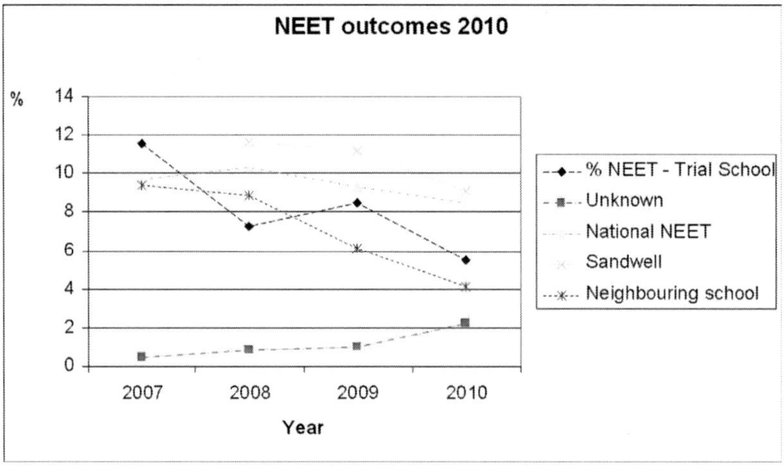

Figure 4.3: NEET outcomes 2007-2010

With only a small number of NEET students in the cohort it was possible to analyse the outcomes for each category of student. The categories were as follows:

No risk factors	(WRF = 0)
Low	(WRF between 1 and 5)
Medium	(WRF between 6 and 9)
High	(WRF >9)

Figure 4.4 plots the percentage of those who are NEET in each group against an estimate of how many people would probably have ended up in this category without intervention. These figures were only estimated for the high-risk group and must be treated with extreme caution. We are not claiming to be rigorous here, but it should be noted that no claims have been made for any other group – only for those who were high-risk.

If these – highly speculative – ideas can indeed be validated, it would suggest that it is possible to work with the most vulnerable groups in a highly positive way.

There was an additional and unexpected benefit. All the young people in the high-risk group were visited at home by the Connexions personal adviser. A visit to one boy's house found that he was not attending school nor living at home with his mother. The Connexions personal adviser persisted and found the boy living at a friend's house. The boy was not attending school because of an incident involving mobile phones. As a consequence of his non-attendance the school had withdrawn his work experience placement and the boy was effectively lost to the educational system.

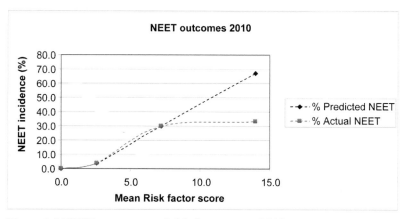

Figure 4.4 NEET outcomes and risk factor group 2010

The boy's low attendance level would probably have attracted attention eventually, but the agencies involved in maintaining the welfare of young people all had their own *individual* thresholds for intervention. The cumulative nature of the NEET screening method allowed the following pupils to be highlighted: those whose primary care, school attendance levels, living situations, and health might be cause for some concern, but not enough to warrant an intervention by the individual agencies working with such children. In the boy's case, social services investigated what was an informal fostering arrangement and provided the necessary safeguards and his work experience placement resumed and further alternative provision was put in place. It is unlikely that such provision would have been allocated had the boy not been part of the screening programme.

Known vulnerable groups

That we have not included certain groups who are known to be vulnerable might come as something of a surprise. The model does highlight individuals from such groups as looked-after and young carers. The following case study has been contributed by Ana Aparicio from the team for Looked After Children in Education (LACE).

The LACE team decided to explore the NEET model further after listening to a presentation in which it was stated that, in one local authority at least, being looked after was not a factor that increases a person's risk of not being in education, employment, or training in the future. The LACE team considered a number of factors that might have led to this conclusion. One considered, for example, that the looked-after children in the pilot cohort might have been in stable education and had secure home settings. Another identified that certain risk factors – for example, unemployment in family, changes in accommodation, and poor basic skills did not necessarily have the same currency for looked-after children. This is discussed in more detail in the section 'adapting the model'.

In the first instance the LACE team wanted to test the model out to see if the results it generated for a particular year group tallied with the staff's knowledge of the children.

Running the original model

We tested the model with a cohort of Year 9 pupils who were looked-after. There were 39 children in all. Running the model was straightforward. Two members of the LACE team were involved: one sat at a computer with access to the database and the other sat at a computer with a spreadsheet containing the risk factors and the children's names. Information such as last change of address could be quickly verified by finding details on the database, and staff's own knowledge of individual children. Zero or 1 was then put into the spreadsheet in the appropriate box. Where neither of the two LACE staff had sufficient knowledge of a child and the database could not provide the necessary information, the rest of the team were consulted. In only a few instances was it necessary to clarify a particular detail about a child with another team member.

Once the process was complete a data set was produced in which each child was given a weighting just as they were in the original study. We hypothesized that a child's weighting correlated with how at risk they were of not being in education, employment, or training in the future. So, for those with a low weighting the risk would be low; for those with a high weighting the risk would be high. The table of results was then shown to the LACE team who were asked to evaluate the data and say whether they agreed with the findings. For example, where a child had a low weighting, did this correspond with their knowledge of the child? And vice versa: where a child had a high weighting, was this someone that a member or members of the team were significantly concerned about?

Findings

It was unanimously agreed that the model produced accurate information. There were no major discrepancies between how the data identified the children as being at high, medium, or low risk – and how the staff would have classified them themselves. Any changes they would have made related to only two children: the first was considered to be more at risk by staff but was weighted as being third most at risk by the data; the second was given a weighting of 1 that did not correspond with the staff's view that the child had a zero risk at that time. In both cases, however, each child remained in the same groupings identified in the original model.

The table summarizes the scores for the looked-after children, comparing them to those who participated in the original model. Compared with 40 per cent of all children, as many as 84 per cent looked-after had weightings of at least one or more. Since 35 per cent scored six or more compared with only 9 per cent of all children – it would seem that looked-after children are at an increased risk of becoming NEET if they are not prioritized for support.

Table 4.9: Risk factor scores for looked-after children and all children

Weightings	All (%)	Looked-after (%)
0	60	16
1–5	31	49
6–9	6	24
10+	3	11

Adapting the model

Certain headings in the original model did not have the same currency for looked-after children as they did for those who are not. We are therefore looking to draw up a 'looked-after' version of the model, using the same sequence it employed to test out the findings that arose. The 'looked-after' model might address some of the difficulties they encountered. For instance, the original model gives a weighting of 1 to poor basic skills – but the importance of good basic skills in an unstable family environment is likely to be greater than the case in one more stable. The LACE team suggested that a higher weighting would be more appropriate.

Another heading that presented difficulties was 'unemployment in family'. For looked-after children this raised the question of which family should be considered: the one they were born into or their foster or residential family? It was decided that it should be the former, as many children would not have access to that particular information. If the latter were considered, their employment status would lead to no differentiation between the cohort.

'Accommodation issues' is a further heading that the LACE team would like to adapt. For the purposes of trying out the model we decided that if any child had changed address in the previous six months, they would be given a score of 1.

Future work

The LACE team have already run the current model in other year groups. The risk factor scores are being cross-matched with other information about the allocation of resources to individual children: those with the highest risks are receiving more services than those with lower risk-factor scores. Any follow-on work has to be responsive as a looked-after child's level of instability often changes rapidly and professionals working with such children need to be able to react accordingly.

The LACE team would also like to use the model retrospectively, running it, for example, in a Year 11 cohort to see how many might have changed risk groups according to what staff knew about them when they were in Year 7. Of particular interest would be those students whom staff considered to be at high risk in Year 7 and whose risk-factor score had lowered as they progressed through the school. Unpicking which factors contributed to such changes might then inform future practice.

Conclusion

Though the model suggests that the risk of entering the NEET category is higher for looked-after children, this does not imply that this particular factor is, in itself, determining. That these children are at a high risk of entering the NEET category comes not from being looked-after, but from the higher incidence of instability that characterizes this cohort.

If we accept that entering the NEET category is a legitimate indication of vulnerability, the screening at least three years before this happens can be justified if reductions are seen. We suggest that current practice fails to take into account what evidence makes clear: around half the children at risk of becoming NEET can be identified three years earlier. We also suggest that the risk can be reduced if an early link is established with a Connexions personal adviser.

An unexpected benefit of using a cumulative method lies in its capacity to identify young people whose situations don't quite meet thresholds for intervention by individual agencies but lead to a high degree of vulnerability. The method clearly has not been developed with this goal in mind and therefore it needs to be investigated in significantly greater detail. The Common Assessment Framework (CAF) performs a similar function for individuals and the screening method might highlight those whose situations may warrant a CAF investigation.

This study has shown that screening for NEET status at least three years before statutory school leaving is possible. When used it can ensure that resources are targeted earlier and, in particular, stabilizing relationships – which can act as reference points for the transition between school and work – are developed. If such relationships are established in time – before disaffection with school has become irreversible and pupils have grown distrustful of agencies – we will undoubtedly improve the outcomes for the most vulnerable children. We argue that this approach offers better value for money than attempts to re-engage students once disaffection has become chronic.

Chapter 5

Introduction to case studies – the realities

Throughout our careers we have had contact with many young people who have not been in education, employment, or training, as well as with their families, through various institutions. Having met and worked with such young people, we have become particularly interested in finding out more about them and the events that might have affected them. Though we provide support to young people in our current roles, we do not always have access to all the relevant information regarding them and surmised that this would probably be the case for other professionals with whom they are involved. Each person, as a consequence, might have a slightly different outlook depending on what information is available to them.

The case studies presented in this book are our attempt to represent several different perspectives on a person who has been in the NEET category. In the hope that we might demonstrate the bigger picture, we talked to several key members in that person's life to ascertain what the situation was like from their point of view.

The approach we have used to research NEET is supported by key concepts regarding objectivity and subjectivity. The word 'research' might conjure up a laboratory experiment where we manipulate factors under controlled conditions to observe the effects of those manipulations. Such an approach might be useful for objects that are constant. For example, if we apply heat to water, we know it will boil as the temperature reaches 100^0 centigrade. We also know that the boiling point will be affected by specific factors like atmospheric pressure. As we know the relationship between boiling point and atmospheric pressure, we can predict with a large amount of certainty what the boiling point will be under specific atmospheric conditions. Here, we are working with predictable cause–effect relationships. In such cases, knowledge is generated by being objective and scientific.

We assume that reality is equally subject to predictable rules and can therefore be measured objectively. If we applied factors such as the time of day or the day of the week they would be irrelevant to the boiling point. We are enjoined to ask how we are able to research what people think or feel. Each person has their own view and perspective shaped by the experiences they have had. What one person thinks about a situation may therefore differ completely from another person's interpretation of the same situation. This is the *subjective* element. Working with people's views as subjects might be problematic. When looking at a concept like NEET we have been unable to produce a one-size-fits-all theory, since each individual is affected by different factors and has individual reasons for why they became NEET.

Why are we looking at the risk factors connected to becoming NEET? While some research enquires into causal relationships between different factors, other research aims to illuminate complex situations with the intention of increasing understanding between people. In cases like ours where the 'subjects' are people, we accept that while it is impossible to produce an objective, predictive solution, by providing information about the risk factors of becoming NEET we might help identify preventative measures.

To complete our research, we used a *phenomenological* approach that is 'expressly interested in people's experiences and particularly the experiences of those people who are usually ignored' (Levering, 2006: 457). This book aims to continue this approach by presenting the stories of young people who have been NEET, who themselves feel strongly about their stories being heard. The accounts are told verbatim from the participant's perspective but to further incorporate the views often ignored, we have included accounts of their parents and other key individuals connected with them.

Phenomenology has its roots in philosophy from the work of two principal theorists: Edmund Husserl (1859–1938) and Martin Heidegger (1889–1976). Husserl is sometimes known as the father of phenomenology for combining a number of concepts into a unified theory. He introduces the concept of *Lebenswelt* (Husserl, 1936), which translates as 'lived experience' and suggests that phenomenology involves describing experiences. Husserl's phenomenology emphasizes that the researcher should have few preconceptions and should look at the common features of lived experience (Lopez and Willis, 2004). He terms the restraint of preconceptions 'bracketing', a process that involves suspending subjectivity and not making judgements or assumptions. Interpretation is a key feature in Heidegger's phenomenology. He introduces the concept of *Dasein* (Heidegger, 1927), or 'being in the world'. *Dasein* is not just about lived experience as Husserl suggested, but involves the meaning of being. Rejecting the idea of bracketing, Heidegger focused on the reflection and interpretation of experience and argued that it was impossible to be fully objective. The important context in his work is the *relationship* to the *Lebenswelt*, rather than the *Lebenswelt* itself.

Phenomenological approaches to research are typically found in family therapy and healthcare. In such areas, it is important for professionals to understand the way individuals experience situations. For example, Dyson (2005) points out that while there might be agreement about what asthma is, this does not mean that everyone who has the condition expresses it identically. Stubblefield and Murray (2002) use a phenomenological approach to help understand mental illness. Considering family therapy, meanwhile, Sprenkle makes a further contribution. He refers to 'storytelling' as a means of looking at how each family member might make sense of a family event: 'just as family therapists do, phenomenological family researchers must elicit the perceptions and views of all family members to get the total picture of a particular family' (Sprenkle, 2005: 66).

In a similar way our project aimed to elicit the views of a range of individuals involved in one phenomenon: NEET. To illustrate its complexity, we used case studies to look at the topic from a broad perspective but within each case study we considered risk factors and the stories of key individuals.

To identify potential participants and remain aligned with a phenomenological approach, we undertook purposive sampling, obtaining a sample of participants by selection according to specific characteristics. We wanted to identify young people who had been NEET at some point after they had left compulsory education. The sample involved a certain amount of hand-picking to ensure that participants were both male and female and from more than one ethnic background and included young people willing to participate.

In terms of research associated with phenomenology, the principal method is an unstructured interview, which allows participants to recall their experiences freely. This is preferable to a structured interview that has 'a standard format of pre-determined questions in a set order' or a 'semi-structured interview which involves the interviewer deciding in advance what broad topics are to be covered and what main questions are to be asked' (Miller and Brewer, 2003: 167). We chose an unstructured interview to avoid participants feeling restricted by the researcher's questions; the method gives them free rein in recalling their experience. We also asked participants to comment and reflect on their experiences, adding an extra dimension to the descriptions that Denscome (2003) emphasizes in phenomenological research.

Continuing with this approach, we carried out unstructured interviews with key individuals involved with the young person who has been NEET, including parent/s, a key worker from the young person's school, a Connexions personal adviser, and any other fundamental figures. Such individuals might include, for instance, learning mentors, partners, or professionals from other institutions. The interviews were recorded and transcribed. Each account was then edited to make it anonymous and eliminate repetition. All words used were those of the participants and the transcription method faithfully reproduced the language they used, including dialect. Where this might lead to difficulties with interpretation, footnotes give clarification.

To analyse and interpret the research, we followed a Husserlian view and took the comments of Groenewald (2004) into account. Groenewald sees the notion of 'data analysis' as running counter to the phenomenological approach, since analysis implies a breaking-down of data that might then interfere with presenting the phenomenon. Groenewald prefers the term 'explicitation'. In light of this, we felt that idea to be of greater benefit than a detailed analysis to highlight the risk factors surrounding NEET.

However, we have considered Giorgi's (1994) three steps for a phenomenological method:

- description: giving a precise account
- reduction: the researcher takes a step back from the topic (similar to the process of bracketing)
- search for essences: where the characteristics of the phenomenon are examined so that 'essential' characteristics are identified.

From this we try, in the final chapter, to identify some common risk factors from the case studies and use these to make suggestions that might help in identifying ways of preventing young people becoming NEET.

Ethical issues

Throughout the project we refer to guidance from the British Psychological Society (BPS, 2004) and the British Educational Research Association (BERA, 2004). The guidance provides the basis for maintaining the correct conduct when working with vulnerable individuals, since our research involved interviews focusing on issues surrounding young people, some of whom were under the age of 18. We also gained informed voluntary consent from all the key individuals and ensured confidentiality throughout.

In accordance with the guidelines detailed above, the case studies presented have been anonymized so none of the individuals can be identified. However, we realized that each individual who took part in the case study would be able to recognize their own and others' contributions, which might possibly hurt or cause offence if individuals disagreed. To prevent this arising, we obtained the consent of individuals in two ways. We initially obtained consent to carry out the interview and to tape record it. Once transcribed, each interviewee was sent a copy not only of the transcript of their own interview but also all the other transcripts in the case study so they could give feedback about any material they preferred not to be included in the final edited case study. Such material could be information they considered untrue or didn't want shared in print. We agreed to remove any unwanted material without question. Following this opportunity, each individual was asked to sign a consent form agreeing to the case study being included in the book. Once the consent form was signed, no alterations were made to the case study. If the person was under the age of 18, we obtained consent from their parents as well.

By sending the interviewees their individual transcripts and edited case studies we added to their validity – or what Groenewald refers to as 'validity and truthfulness' in phenomenological research. The process gave participants an opportunity to see what they had said, to reflect on it and then, if they felt it appropriate, to give feedback to the authors – a step that increased confidence in each case study's authenticity while simultaneously addressing the ethical issues.

Chapter 6

Tim

Tim is white, speaks English as his first language and was raised by his birth parents. Tim's mother left the family when he was 14 and he now lives with his father who is not currently working. Tim occasionally helps his father with casual work, often using the family's pickup truck.

Tim's risk-factor score was 10, from:

Known to the youth offending team (YOT)
Low motivation
Unemployment in the family
Poor behaviour in school
LDD (he was on the SEN code of practice)
Poor school attendance

Interviews were conducted with Tim and his father in their home. The second interviewer was a Connexions personal adviser, Tracey Baker, who was known to the family. Interviews were also conducted with his allocated Connexions personal adviser, the manager of the school's Centre of Inclusion, and the school's head of inclusion, an assistant head who knew Tim. For the purposes of this text, the school has been named Ridgeacre.

Timeline for Tim

Date	*Activity*
Sept 2005	
Sept 2006	
Sept 2007	
Sept 2008	Compulsory education
Sept 2009	
Sept 2010	
Aug 2011	
Sept 2011	
Oct 2011	
Nov 2011	College
Dec 2011	
Jan 2012	
Feb 2012	
Mar 2012	
Apr 2012	NEET
May 2012	
June 2012 – to date	

Tim's story

Interviewer: We are here to talk about your time at Ridgeacre High and we want to take you back to the early days in Ridgeacre, perhaps Year 7. What was it like? What do you remember about it?

Tim: Horrible.

Interviewer: Right.

Tim: Absolutely horrible.

Interviewer: What were the bits that were particularly horrible?

Tim: Well, you're a young kid in a big school, ain't ya. So you got older kids bullying ya, you got older kids saying stuff to ya and you got people you don't know that want to prove their self.

Interviewer: So, horrible, I mean you're smiling when you say horrible, so I guess there were some funny sides to it as well.

Tim: Yeah.

Interviewer: Were there any good bits?

Tim: Dunno, it's been that long. There probably wor[1] but I cor[2] remember 'um.[3]

Interviewer: Do you remember any particular teachers or staff?

Tim: Um, I do but there's a few.

Interviewer: OK. Do you remember any from the Centre of Inclusion?

Tim: Yeah, I know um all.

Interviewer: Who do you remember from there?

Tim: Miss Barnes, Miss Atton, Mr Sindhu, um, Miss Haynes, Miss Harper obviously and a few others as well.

Interviewer: Right, OK. And what do you remember about spending your time at the Centre of Inclusion?

Tim: That was horrible, horrible, just horrible.

Interviewer: So what was horrible about it?

Tim: Dunno, just the way, the way it works up there. I just day[4] like school, full stop.

Interviewer: Right. During the time you were at school, what did you think you would do when you left?

[Pause]

Interviewer: Any ideas?

---

[1] were
[2] can't
[3] them
[4] didn't

Tim: Become an electrician – well at first it was a paint and body repairer on vehicles but I just couldn't get nowhere. Then it was an electrician I wanted to be.

Interviewer: And did you get into trouble at school?

Tim: Oh yeah [laughs], loads.

Interviewer: What sort of trouble did you get into?

Tim: All sorts: vandalism, fighting, anything you can think of, anything that went against the school's code of conduct. Bit of everything, really, just mischievous.

Interviewer: Can you remember any one particular thing that got you into trouble?

Tim: God, there's bin⁵ that many. Probably fighting and back chatting probably the most. And then I stopped going to school after a bit. I stopped. I only went in for half of Year 11.

Interviewer: And you obviously got away with that?

Tim: Oh yeah.

Interviewer: So how did you manage that?

Tim: Stay out the way of the teacher, avoid her.

Interviewer: OK, and did you get any certificates for any exams or anything?

Tim: Well, I got a few GCSEs, I got two, well four GCSEs but two at a C grade. Um, got some level 2s which I don't know which they are and I got other certificates and that.

Interviewer: Towards the end, were there people there that were pushing you towards training, jobs, or staying on at school? Were there any people around like that?

Tim: Can you say again?

Interviewer: Towards the end; towards Year 10 and 11.

Tim: Oh yeah.

Interviewer: Were people saying, why don't you do this, why don't you do that if you want to become an electrician?

Tim: Not really, I was just in trouble. They used to talk to me about my behaviour rather than my career.

Interviewer: So did you have people talk to you about careers?

Tim: Ah, yeah, only a couple of times. I forgot their names, they wor from Connexions. It was only about three or four times and that was it, helped me get into college which I dain't⁶ stop on at.

---

⁵ been
⁶ didn't

Interviewer: Well let's just talk about that. I suppose before we do, were you always living here?

Tim: Yeah, I have always lived here.

Interviewer: OK. And did you ever get into trouble with the police?

Tim: Couple of times.

Interviewer: Right.

Tim: I don't really get into trouble when I'm out, if you know what I mean. I don't go around the streets; I just go round to a mate's house and that. When I was a kid I used to get in trouble.

Interviewer: And is your dad in work?

Tim: Um, no, I don't know.

Interviewer: OK. And was he in work while you were at school?

Tim: Um, I'm just wondering, like.

Interviewer: Did he have a job?

Tim: At first. When I was in Year 7 and 8.

Interviewer: He had a job, then. OK, fine. You kind of stopped attending school, certainly full-time, in Year 11. What happened when you left?

Tim: Um.

Interviewer: At the end of Year 11.

Tracey Baker (TB): Where did you go?

Tim: Straight to college.

Interviewer: Which college?

Tim: Ainsborough, the Olton one it was though.

Interviewer: That's OK. What course did you do there?

Tim: Um, painting on body of vehicles, but I couldn't stop on it 'cause I needed an apprenticeship, like a job, but I couldn't get a job.

Interviewer: So did you complete? Do a whole year there?

Tim: No, I never did it; I did, like, six weeks.

TB: Did you do the training bit of it – the pre-training bit – and then you couldn't stay on unless …

Tim: No, I couldn't. It was a course like an apprenticeship course.

TB: So you needed a placement to stay on?

Tim: Yeah.

TB: And you couldn't find a placement?

Tim: No.

TB: OK.

Interviewer: So what happened then? You just stopped?

Tim: Yeah, yeah.

Interviewer: OK, so then what happened?

Tim: Stayed sitting at home all day, playing my Xbox.

[Laughs].

Interviewer: So what's happening now? Has that been the case ever since?

Tim: Well, yeah it has, yeah.

Interviewer: I saw you out yesterday with your dad and Dad says you go out with him.

Tim: It ain't really going out – it's just, sitting about ay[7] it.

Interviewer: So at the moment?

Tim: I just go out, pop out in the day. I don't work or nothing.

Interviewer: Right. So how long have you not been working?

Tim: I ain't had a job, have I, really.

Interviewer: No, OK.

Tim: 'Cause I been at college; well, I was at college.

Interviewer: So you stopped college, was it last October?

Tim: Something like that. Nah it might have been about January – well I cor[8] remember.

TB: After the six weeks?

Tim: Probably, yeah.

TB: Do you want to work?

Tim: I want a career – an apprenticeship more than anything.

TB: Has anybody tried to support you in finding that?

Tim: Um, not really. I've been up Connexions but it's just you need grades to hire people. The companies want grades and I ain't got 'um to give 'em.

Interviewer: OK. How do you see the next year?

Tim: Difficult.

TB: You know when you were at school and you did your work, how did you find the work when you were there?

Tim: Horrible, everything was just horrible about school. I don't like talking about it.

TB: Did you find it difficult to do the work?

Tim: Not really.

TB: You just weren't interested in it?

Tim: [Shakes his head.]

Interviewer: Think we'll probably stop there. Is there anything else you want to say about school that you remember?

---

[7] isn't
[8] can't

Tim: Nah, that's it really.

Interviewer: Thank you very much.

Tim's father's story

Interviewer: Right, we're here to talk about your son Tim and we're leading up to the time when he left school but we want to start really with his experience at school. He went to Ridgeacre. What do you remember? What were your experiences of Tim at school?

D: Well, I'll be honest, I was always at work. I suppose that's the easiest cop out ain't it, for anything. Um, I never really had a lot of time to obviously go down to the school 'cause his mother always went down to the school, you know, whenever he had his problems. Um, phew, I knew he had problems at school; he had problems at school from the time long before he went to Ridgeacre. I think when he went to Rangers, uh, Days Avenue.

Interviewer: Yeah, Rangers Court.

D: I think it was on Days Avenue, that's right, and, um, there he was always classed as a special child, what they called a special child, where he was always under supervision by a teacher, which I always thought was a bit extreme. But, you know, I always thought they knew best, as you do as a parent. As I say I never had much time for it. Um, but obviously I had to listen to me wife at the time and obviously take her advice on what was going on. And, er, I left it at that, I thought "he's young" but when he went to mainstream school he would always seem to be, I mean, I'll be honest, he always seemed that he needed the attention. He always wanted to be noticed, that's the easiest way I can put it. And maybe they – and obviously maybe the other children pick up on it, I don't know. Basically they gid[9] him an hard time and Tim's one of these that will give 'em a hard time back and it maybe stood him out from the rest. That's the only way I can put it; it's the easiest way to put it. His mother always said he had psychological problems anyway. I never thought that for one minute; I always thought it was his mother.

Interviewer: Right.

D: And it was pointed out how the one time her said to me her had took him for counselling 'cause they always thought he had that ADHD and obviously the counsellor was saying "no he ain't got ADHD", or whatever they call it, and, er, he progressed and progressed and he stopped going a couple of years ago I think. He said that it was she that needed the counselling, not Tim. And her admitted to that herself, I mean, and I think, and I knew

---

[9] gave

that it was because of his mom, 'cause of the way she used to treat him sometimes but we won't go into that.

Interviewer: So were there good things at school as well as things that weren't?

D: Well, obviously he hasn't come out a bad child; actually he's all right. I think he's just getting depressed that he cor[10] get a job; he wants a job but he cor get a job. That's the way, but I don't know how he is gonna mix, he's also had problems mixing with people at school and I sometimes wonder, I mean sometimes I have a difficult time with him. Being a parent you expect it, but he's good round me, you know, he's good for me – maybe I'm good for him, I don't know, but we get on, you know what I mean. And, um, I'm just a bit worried that when he goes into, when he eventually does get a job, will he be able to hold down a job? With, you know, 'cause he has got a temper on him and sometimes he'll, he'll listen to other people but he won't listen to me. Even if, when I'm trying to point him in the right direction, if you understand what I'm trying to say. As I said before, I've never had that in my life. I had to find out the hard way, but then again I worn't[11] a problem child [laughs], if you know what I'm trying to say.

Interviewer: So are you in work at the moment?

D: No, I just, er, do a little bit of this and a little bit of that just to survive. I keep my head, I take Tim with me when I can. I move a bit of furniture, a bit of this and a bit of that and collect wood. I'm happy with that; I'm at home, I feed him, he's all right, as you can see he don't go hungry, the size of him.

Interviewer: Has he been in trouble with the police at all?

D: He's had a couple of scrapes with 'em. But nothing that I can say represents trouble. When I was his age, well, when I was a lot younger than him and his age, when I was about 12-ish, 10, 12, 14, I was always in trouble with the police. The police was always knocking on my mother's door. But then again, it was for me brothers as well. It was the time when my mother hadn't got a penny, well, how do I put this, well they ain't got no money and it was hard times then and he don't know hard times that what I've had. And I sometimes wish we could go back that way and maybe it might teach 'em a lesson, no I do, but he's gettin' there, I can honestly say that he is. He don't, he ain't brought the coppers back. Well, about 12 or 18 months ago – the police told him he was in a place he shouldn't be. I gave him a clout round the ear while the copper was there, I did, as big as he is, but he learnt. I think

---

[10] can't
[11] wasn't

he's learnt his lesson that that ain't the way forward; but no, honestly no, he ain't brought, no he ay. I've seen a lot worse than Tim, a lot, lot, worse and he's polite to people and he is.

Interviewer: Yes, you can see that. How's his reading, writing and number?

D: He's all right, he's – as far as I know he's reading and writing OK. I mean, he has times in everything he does, obviously, as I said before, I'm a dinosaur. Tim ay, he's young, he's bin brought up with mobile phones, computers, you know. There was nothing like that when I was at school. And I was thick at school.

Interviewer: He's said to us that in his last year at school, he didn't go all the time.

D: No, he probably did not, no, 'cause he day enjoy goin' to Greensmill. I used to get onto him and say look, just go, Tim. But I never really had any comebacks off the people that, you know, the lecturers or teachers or whoever was the guidance, no. I mean, he said he had problems there, you know, with a few people, obviously, where they wanna, like kids do, they bicker don't they? Someone says boo, you say boo back and Tim is like that. He's like his mother and me elder lad is more like me. He's more laid back, Tim ain't. He's forward, he won't let anyone put him down. Someone tries to put him down and he'll put 'em down back himself. Maybe it's a good thing, maybe it's a bad thing, I don't know.

TB: Was going to Greensmill an opportunity suggested by Ridgeacre?

D: I don't really know because as I say, me wife dealt with all that and I'll be honest, guilty as sin, I day always listen, I was clocked off – maybe a bad thing, I don't know.

Interviewer: So what do you think is going to happen to him?

D: Well, I got to be honest, I'm hoping, I mean, when he went to that job down at Kwik Fit he got through to the, like, interview stage. They sent him a rail ticket to go down to sort himself out but I don't think he's got the confidence to go down on the train on his own. I am being, you know, he did say to me he could do it but he said to me, he said, "Dad can you tek[12] me?", so I had to tek him to Kinghay. So I run him into Kinghay and he directed me in – so he can read a map, he ain't that thick either. And we got there and he was quite happy and content with what he'd showed 'em and he said to me, he said, "I was outshining 'em". They give you a manual test from what he was telling me; you know, um, a hands-on sort of thing. He said, "Dad, I flew through it," he said, "I flew through it and I was finished before they was,

---

[12] take

even", you know, the people that was there, out of the 10 people that was there, he said, "I was finished before them". You know, and he says "because I could d'that – it's easy for me". And he is, he is always fidgeting, and he is, I used to say, wire that plug up and he would wire the plug up. He is, you know, he ay – as I said before he ain't thick, he's far from thick but at the same time it comes down to, and I says this to him, it's the grades that am[13] letting ya down at the end of the day. I've said, and this is when I get onto him again, I say look, this is, and I do, I say because you know what it was, because you DID NOT listen to what we was telling ya about getting grades at school. Then sometimes the old sh, sh, sh, comes out then, and it does, you know what I mean. But as I say you can only give credit to your children some of the time, not all of the time – you'll learn that lesson yourself one day.

Interviewer: [Laughs] I don't think so. I think we have probably got what we need. That's it. Is there anything else you want to say?

D: No, you're all right, you've asked me and I've, well, I've given you an honest, best honest answer I can give ya.

Interviewer: That's what we want.

D: As I said, I've always been there for me children but I've got him all the time now since his mom's gone. He's calmed down a lot since his mom's gone. He is still in touch with his mom, you know, it's peaceful, it's quiet.

Centre of Inclusion manager's story

Interviewer: Let's go back to your earliest memories of Tim.

D: Tim through his lower school years, through Key Stage 3, had one or two minor behaviour issues and he had one or two stints up in isolation for, excuse the pun, "tomfoolery" more than anything else. His behaviour started to decline sort of Year 9 time, which is why we identified him as one of the candidates to go on our alternative provision in Year 10 and 11. But yeah, through his lower school he was very calm and very peaceful and then Year 9 was a bit of a nose dive, so from then on we kept him.

Interviewer: How would you describe his basic skills?

D: Tim, rather frustratingly, was extremely bright. I remember having many conversations with him about the fact that actually things came very easily to him, while a lot of the other students who are on our alternative provision struggle on a daily basis. He used to pick things up straight away and understand what needed to be done; he could write pages and pages of beautifully written and very well expressed, er, English work. He was a very talented young man but he chose not to use those talents; he'd much rather

---

[13] are

sit idle and either avoid doing anything at all or come up with ailments or excuses for anything that he possibly could to avoid doing any work.

Interviewer: OK. Was he on your Special Needs register?

D: Erm, yes, I think he was under school action and that was going to be because of behaviour. As I say, it was the main decline in Year 9 that we saw. That was the thing that first introduced him to the SEN register.

Interviewer: How would you describe his motivation? Did he have ambitions?

D: Yeah, he was always aiming towards something and it was always sort of to do with cars, er, he very much enjoyed tinkering around under the hood with his dad. He would come in after the weekend glowing and filling us in on every tiny detail of what they'd done on the weekend under the bonnet of their van. And it was very clear that that was what he wanted to do; he was very much into everything, or his versions; when he was sitting at school he would tell us some yarns about what he'd been doing at the weekend and he'd been out tatting,[14] he'd been doing this, that, and the other. So, yeah, he was always full of stories, which actually in the end started to cause some friction between him and the rest of the group. There was an element of… he used to embellish some of these stories and the group very quickly picked up on that. A lot of the time he would start telling one of his yarns, and I can remember quite clearly the other students would say, "oh god, here goes Tim again" and "here's another one of Tim's stories". Towards the end they actually, they stopped tolerating it and there were a few fallings out over it that we then needed to sort out.

Interviewer: What kind of stories are we talking about? What kinds of things would he embellish?

D: Oh he'd always, he'd come in and say that he'd been involved with this, that, the other. He'd do a very big list of places he'd been to or, well, some of these stories just didn't ring true, er, and the kids obviously knew that so that used to cause problems.

Interviewer: Did he get involved with the police or the youth offending team at all?

D: I think at some point he did, I can't recall for why, though. I think at some point, yes, the police were involved with some of the stuff he was getting involved with out of school.

Interviewer: What was his attendance like?

D: At one point very good and then towards the end very hit and miss. He didn't have a very happy and positive relationship with the school. He

---

[14] Collecting and selling scrap metal

didn't enjoy it; he tolerated it, I think is probably the best way to describe his relationship with school. More often than not when he found himself in bother, he needed to be pulled up for something or other, he wouldn't be, he would avoid school like the plague in the vain hope that we would forget whatever mischief he'd gotten into, and he could come back into school like nothing had happened, so yeah.

Interviewer: Were you aware of any unemployment in the family?

D: Yes, I think Dad was having problems with unemployment and I think there were issues at home anyway between Mom and Dad. I think that started around Year 9, which obviously went hand in hand with the decline in his behaviour. Obviously, from Tim's point of view, he very much came from a stable family home, was idolized to the point of being spoilt by his parents, which again caused a lot of problems. The lack of work and Dad's lack of drive and motivation, because obviously he'd been looking for jobs for a long period of time, he became very disheartened. I think it had an impact on Tim in a positive way, interestingly, because Tim got to spend more time with him as he was at home. He appreciated this quite a lot and obviously his relationship with his dad strengthened. He worships his dad. Problems arose with his relationship with his mom because, obviously, of his good relationship with his dad. He veered off towards his dad's side and Mom used to get it in the neck quite a lot. A lot of the meetings I'd had when I went round to the house, Mom would sit and be there but towards the end he didn't really have any respect for his mom, so that became quite difficult.

Interviewer: Did he manage to finish school here?

D: He did, er, yes, he managed to claw his way through, not necessarily with grades that he was capable of achieving, but again that came down to his motivation. A lot of the peer stuff that went on – he had very few friends, he was quite a solitary young man, erm, mainly because of the stories and the yarns that he used to spin. But also he chose to be quite solitary, actually a lot; it was a decision that he made. His grades I was quite disappointed with; he could have achieved so much more, erm, but I don't think... I think he would have had the opportunity and he would have looked into redoing some of his GCSEs at college, but again I think that his lack of motivation means that he's never actually gotten round to doing that.

Interviewer: What did he go on to after school?

D: Erm, we did hear, obviously aunt works in the school and she keeps us informed with some of the stuff that's he's up to. He did have appointments with Connexions and placements at colleges were sort of made under the kind of motor vehicle umbrella.

Interviewer: He was always very interested in the bodywork side of things and the painting and the sprays that they do. Whether he actually followed that through I doubt, but it still remained his ambition to do something with cars. Recently I know he went for an interview with Kwik Fit and had to go through their interview process but I don't think that's come to anything either.

Assistant principal's story

Interviewer: Before we start talking about Tim, what's your role here?

R: I'm senior assistant principal and I oversee pastoral and inclusion.

Interviewer: Brilliant, and we're here to talk about Tim. Basically what do you remember about him?

R: Tim really was a quite multi-faceted young man, really, I think you could say. Erm, he was quite a bright young man, could be mature, helpful, sensible and he could work hard on occasions. The flip side to him was that he was also a very aggressive young man; he was probably one of the hardest people that I've tried to engage in work. He had huge problems getting on with other students, mainly down to the fact that he liked to talk about what he'd done and where he'd been and what he was going to do. And the other kids knew that he was just making it all up and it all then used to fall apart and they'd take the mickey out of him. He'd upend tables and threaten to kill them and do all sorts of terrible things and that really was the biggest factor in the inability for him to access the mainstream school.

Interviewer: What were the developments between Year 7 and 11? How did things change, do you think?

R: At the time as he was moving through, the Centre of Inclusion was really just starting to come into its own and he ended up on one of our alternative provision courses for his Key Stage 4, which was really what stopped him from being permanently excluded. There were, in fact, during Year 9, a number of occasions when he could have been excluded for his violent outbursts but we managed to maintain him with us in the Centre. And in Year 10 he actually did quite well, erm, on the alternative curriculum and then in Year 11 his attendance tapered off – there were problems at home that also impacted on what was going on in his life. His falling out with other people increased and therefore he engaged less and less as we went through Year 11, er, but he did make it to the end.

Interviewer: What motivated him? Did he have any idea of what he wanted to do when he left?

R: Erm, yeah, he was a very hands-on person, you know, tinkering with anything; if he could take it apart and put it together again he was quite happy. And I think at home he did a lot of things like that and he was very, sort of, handy around the house. But in terms of trying to get himself onto an apprenticeship, he didn't connect with the idea of needing the academic side to enable him to do the practical side of it. We never sort of managed to marry those two together enough, really, for him to be successful because he could have been successful, undoubtedly.

Interviewer: Did he ever get into any trouble with the police?

R: Er, yeah, yeah, there were a couple of things, not anything major I don't think but for a couple of silly things out and about. And again I think that was due in part to the breakdown of the family set-up. In fact, his aunt works here and she took him into her home at one point, to try and ease things and keep him on the straight and narrow, and he actually got on well with her and was considerably different with her than he was at home with Mom.

Interviewer: You did manage to hold onto him and I remember there was a chance that he would be excluded, permanently. He was on a list of pupils at risk. To what do you attribute the success of keeping him in school?

R: Er, I think the set-up that we've got here, that enabled him to have his outbursts up here, er, but away from the mainstream of school so other people weren't witnessing it, and therefore we could deal with it in a way that we felt was better for him. But, you know, if we'd left him out in mainstream and he was chucking tables around classrooms and all the rest of it then, you know, we wouldn't really have had an option. So I think that if we hadn't had the Centre of Inclusion then it would have been very difficult to keep hold of him and the staff up here are all very calm and, you know, deal with that sort of behaviour in a very calm manner that enables us to sort of get through it.

Interviewer: Is there anything else that you can remember about Tim?

R: He got on better with adults than other kids and a lot of that was because, as adults, you would listen to all his boastings and just nod really, where kids are intolerant of what they think is patently lies. So he always got on much better with staff. If we could have had him a room on his own, just with the member of staff, we would have never had problems with him at all. It was only when he had to interact with others, and he had a very short fuse, erm, which obviously the others sort of picked up on fairly quickly, erm, and then they used that. It was very difficult to get him to reflect on his own behaviour and how that was having an impact on what was going on in the classroom. He didn't really get what it was that he was doing that was upsetting the others. He knew on occasions and we had times where we would have weeks and weeks of, you know, normality in terms of behaviour and everything, and then it would just all erupt again. You know, it was a case of when he was good he was good, and when he wasn't good he wasn't, bless him [laughs].

Connexions's personal adviser's story

Interviewer: Tell me what contact you had with Tim when he was at school.

PA: Well, I initially met Tim when I gave an introduction about the Connexions service when he was in Year 10. And then throughout Year 11 I supported Tim. At first he was very reluctant to engage or even to speak to me but, erm, 'cause I was based upstairs at Ridgeacre school, upstairs in the Centre of Inclusion and that's where the Connexions office is, and, er, Tim would have a lot of his lessons there, I'd always be bumping into Tim and eventually gained his trust and confidence.

Interviewer: That was good! How long did that take?

PA: Well, er, a couple of weeks, but every time I met Tim he was always really polite and a pleasant lad and he'd always make eye contact with you and then eventually when I started to talk to him about, it's an important year: what are you going to do at the end of Year 11? Slowly he started to engage, especially when I assured him, look, I'm not a social worker, I'm not a counsellor, I'm not a teacher, I'm impartial and I can support you with what it is you want to do.

Interviewer: That sounds good. So you mentioned he spent a lot of time in the Centre of Inclusion. Why did he have lots of his lessons in there?

PA: Well, his attendance was a big issue and also his key and functional skills, so he was really taken out of mainstream and he spent a lot of his lessons up in the Centre of Inclusion. So there was attendance issues and he lacked in confidence as well, a bit of a low motivator, didn't like wearing uniform, always had his cap on as well, you know. But overall he was a really polite and pleasant lad.

Interviewer: Were there any behaviour issues in school that you were aware of?

PA: I think there were one or two behaviour issues; in some lessons he did get agitated and if somebody kicked off then he would answer back and sometimes in the Centre of Inclusion the staff there would be trying to say "come on, Tim, calm down," you know. "You've got to do this, you've got to do your COPE, you've got to finish your coursework off," and sometimes he would have a strop and have time out. But there was a period where I didn't see him for about, erm, I'd say about a good two months. I didn't see him at all and when I did enquire with the Centre of Inclusion staff they said that he's not coming in, he's not attending. Then eventually he did make an appearance and he was put on a reduced timetable, but he was very up and down. Each time I did see him the staff there were very obliging and even though I didn't have an appointment to see Tim, if I had a cancellation I'd go over and say "can I see Tim?." "By all means, Amanda, yes", and that's when I, erm; Tim did eventually engage and say, well, "I like mechanics, I like working with cars", er, and then I told him about training providers, colleges, entry requirements, coursework and there is theory work involved. It is also practical but you are still going to have to do... and build up on your folder. But I did say to him that the support should be there and you should ask for support.

Interviewer: Did he have specific Special Needs?

PA: Not that I'm aware of, I think his basic skills were low, but the staff there, erm, did think that he was more than capable. He was more than capable of finishing any outstanding work and coursework, but there were a few other social issues such as non-attendance, not coming into school. The staff there had done some home visits and he still didn't want to come to school.

Interviewer: Do you think there was a reason?

PA: Not that it was brought to my attention, but then Tim never spoke about anything when I did discuss how things were at home, you know. You really had to – it was like getting blood out of a stone with Tim; it was very short, sharp answers, he would answer back to you, you know. But, yeah, I do believe there were issues going on because all he'd always say to me was, "I want a job, I want a job, I want to do mechanics," and I would say, "well, Tim, you've got to go to college to do that," or "there's training providers" and "how do you feel about college and how do you feel about big groups? Because you don't come to school and you don't like school and you don't like being told what to do, but you're going to have rules all the time." But, then, on a positive, I told him that it would be different from school; the style of learning would be different, his lessons would be different. It wouldn't be five lessons a day, he wouldn't have to wear a uniform, but with mechanics, how did he feel about wearing an overall and heavy shoes? "Yeah, I'm fine and my hands are going to get dirty; yeah, that's what I want to do" and when I did ask him where his interests came from he said he helped out with the family, the cars – helping Dad fix his car and stuff like that.

Interviewer: Did he ever talk about his family at all or anything that might be going on at home?

PA: No, not that I can remember. He may have done but it's been a long time because he's in Year 12 now.

Interviewer: And what happened when he left school? Because you tracked him or tried to track him for a little bit longer.

PA: Yeah, it was difficult to track him down. I mean, near the end of Year 11 when he was coming in and doing his exams, which I was really pleased about, I helped him fill in his online application to college and he said that was where he wanted to go but I told him that he'd have to travel to a nearby town because that's where their mechanics base centre is and he said he was prepared to do that. So, erm, he did his online application, but I noticed while he was doing his application he was very slow on the keyboard and things like writing his name. I told him, "capital letter, start with a capital letter, your postcode, capitals." It was quite funny because throughout he got the hang of it and he'd say, "you're going to say capital letter again, aren't you!" – so it's something I'd picked up on. But then his interview came through one day and he came to tell me in school. He said, "Amanda, my interview came," and then he went to have his interview shortly afterwards. But he was disappointed at one stage because he had to do an assessment at the college and he scored well below average and they, you know, they said he's going to have to start on a Level 1 and he said he was up to Level 2.

Interviewer: So there was a bit of a discrepancy there?

PA: Yeah, the reason being is not only was he on a reduced timetable, he was also on alternative provision. I'm 100 per cent sure he attended one of the training providers with the pre-school provision and that is where he learnt a lot about mechanics as well. And this is where I must give credit to the school, as when they find youngsters who are disengaged and more inclined with practical skills, they do place them with the appropriate provision. But Tim was disappointed, erm, but throughout the activity survey, myself and my colleague Mary, we tried to do our best to track him down. Phone calls – the phone was dead, dead line; letter was sent – no response. We did do home visits – no response. And then one day, because I'm also based in another school and it just so happens that down the road is where Tim was doing Level 2 mechanics, I saw him at the bus stop and so I spoke to him and I said, 'hello Tim', and he was polite and he was with another young person and I said, "how are you?" I could tell he had oil on his hands and he had a rucksack, so I said, "What are you doing here? How are you?" He said, "Oh, I'm at the college, I'm doing mechanics." And he said, "I'm doing Level 2."

Interviewer: Very good.

PA: Yeah. And I said, "Oh that's really good," and he said, "Yeah, they put me onto Level 2," and I said, "Are you enjoying it?" and he said, "Yeah, I got to find a placement, will you help me?" and I said, "I tell you what, come and see us at the centre," and I said, "You know, it's only two minutes away from where you live," and I told him I'm generally in the office on a Friday if it's just me he'd like to see. I said there are advisers that will help him look for a placement. So that was the last time I ever saw and spoke to Tim.

Interviewer: Ah, sounds like you had a bit of a rapport with him?

PA: Yeah, like I said, he was a polite and pleasant lad, not one of these who shy away and after they've left don't come and talk to me and act like they don't know who you are! You know, he was a bubbly lad.

Interviewer: Do you know if he ever got into trouble with the police at all?

PA: No, I don't know about that, not too sure. No, Tim always came across to me that he's the type of young person who might be led, er, easily led into something. But once told about his rights and wrongs he would take it on board, and he never came across as being aggressive or frustrated. You know, maybe perhaps frustrated with things around him; you know, not liking school; not liking some of the students there.

Interviewer: How did he get on with the teachers?

PA: Oh he got on really well with the teachers, yeah, and I've got to give credit to the teachers and the staff at the support centre; they were very supportive, they give them time out and they really look at their needs. If they want one-to-one tuition then they give them that, erm, but he got on well with them. I think it was a couple of students in the Centre of Inclusion; it was a small group in the Centre of Inclusion and all of them had different needs, and so I do recall Tim at times just walking out and pacing up and down the corridor, you know.

Analysis of citations:	
References to low basic skills	1
Low motivation	6
Unemployment in family	2
Poor behaviour in school	7
Known to youth offending team	4
LDD (receiving support)	1
Poor school attendance	9

Chapter 7

Gemma

Gemma is white, speaks English as her first language and was raised by her birth mother. Gemma moved out of her mother's home to live with her boyfriend's family when she was still at school.

Gemma's risk-factor score was 11, arising from:

Changes in accommodation
Low motivation
Unemployment in family
Poor behaviour in school
Low attendance

Interviews were conducted with Gemma and her mother in their home. The school's deputy head was interviewed in school. Gemma's partner David was interviewed, as was her Connexions personal adviser. The school has not been named by any of the interviewees.

Timeline for Gemma

Date	*Activity*
Statutory school leaving	
June 2008	
July 2008	NEET
Aug 2008	
Sept 2008	
Oct 2008	
Nov 2008	
Dec 2008	McDonald's
Jan 2009	
Feb 2009	
March 2009	NEET
April 2009	Juniper
May 2009	NEET
June 2009	
July 2009	
Aug 2009	Confirmed pregnant – NEET
Sept 2009	
Oct 2009	
Nov 2009	
Dec 2009	Teenage parent – NEET
Jan 2010	
Feb 2010	
March 2010	

April 2010	
May 2010	
June 2010	Teenage parent – NEET
July 2010	
Aug 2010	
Sept 2010 – Jan 2011	Confirmed pregnant – NEET
Feb 2011 – to date	

Gemma's story

Interviewer: Right. So what we are going to do is we are just going to have a chat about you, really. So tell me a little bit about school and how that was for you.

Gemma: It was crap, I day[1] like it, I day want to be there. I never used to get out of bed to go there. Never bothered me, day like the teachers.

Interviewer: Was it like that from the start? From Year 7?

Gemma: In Year 7 it was all right, I suppose, and then it was, like, the end of Year 7, I got into, like, mixing with the wrong people and that and I started showing off and doing, like, things and that, do you know what I mean. Just to make myself look clever and stuff.

Interviewer: OK. How did the teachers react to that?

Gemma: Not well, obviously. I used to mess about on purpose to wind them up. So, like, I used to mess about so I knew they would kick me out so I could go and stand outside and mess about even more, do you know what I mean, walk round to other classrooms so that people would see that I was out of class, do you know what I mean.

Interviewer: So when you were there, how did you find the work?

Gemma: All right. I never had a problem with work at all, work wor[2] hard. It wor that work was hard or anything like that. It was just that I couldn't be bothered to do it half the time, but sometimes I did do it and when I did do it it wasn't like a bad, bad, like, do you know what I mean. There wor, it wor crap work I did or nothing like that; I did do all right with my work when I did it.

---

[1] didn't or don't
[2] wasn't

Interviewer: But you just didn't do it some of the time.

Gemma: Yeah.

Interviewer: So attendance at school would have been pretty low?

Gemma: Yeah.

Interviewer: OK. And so what about home? How was home? How did that change as you went through school?

Gemma: When I was in Year 7 I had just moved back in with my mom 'cause I used to live with my nan. And it was like, if I wanted to stay at home, it was all right with my mom, so I could stay at home if I wanted, so I only went to school when I wanted to go to school. I day have to go to school so, do you know what I mean?

Interviewer: Yeah.

Gemma: Well, Year 7, Year 8, I was at school, then Year 9, obviously, I fell out with my mom and that and then I moved in with my boyfriend and lived with him.

Interviewer: So what happened? Do you mind telling me what happened with Mom? What did you fall out with Mom over?

Gemma: When I was in Year 7 and 8 I could do what I wanted to – go to school when I wanted, stay at home when I wanted and then when it was, like, Year 9, the end of Year 9 Mom used to try and say, like, you have got to go to school and if I got suspended, I'd get grounded and then, you know what I mean, you will be in for 9 o'clock and I used to say, "Naa, I'm not coming in for 9 o'clock." I used to try and come in when I wanted to, which means I'd get grounded and then I used to not go back, stay at my boyfriend's instead or have a bust up and go and stay at my nan's.

Interviewer: OK. So while you were in Year 9 and afterwards, you had almost three different addresses and almost three places you could stay?

Gemma: Yeah, it wor like, I didn't get maltreated at home or nothing like that, it's just that Mom went from obviously being not telling me I had to go to school and then, like, all of a sudden trying to make me go to school, do you know what I mean, 'cause school was on her back, and so then, obviously, she used to try and say to me "You am going to school" and I'd be like, "Naa I won't," do you know what I mean. If you are going to make me go to school then I won't be here, I'll move out, and stuff like that.

Interviewer: And so how were Years 10 and 11? When it got to the end how was that?

Gemma: When I was in Year 10, I think it was the end, well about halfway through Year 10 I moved in with my boyfriend properly and stayed at his house. It was, like, I never wanted to go school anyway 'cause I was always at his house. He was just as bad as I was; he was suspended half the time and when he was I wouldn't go anyway, and if we were both there, I'd get suspended and then he'd get suspended 'cause I got suspended, so it was like that.

Interviewer: Was there anything that you remember that got you suspended?

Gemma: Fighting, swearing, answering back – stupid things like, "Gemma, take your jewellery off" or "Gemma, give me your phone," and I'd be like, "You ain't having my phone," do you know what I mean. "You ain't having my phone," and I'd swear at them saying, "You ain't having it, you ain't having my rings." Smoking, wearing my trainers, something stupid like that. When I put my shoes on, I'd have a bust up over it, but I only used to have a bust up to show off.

Interviewer: OK.

Gemma: Do you know what I mean?

Interviewer: Yes. Was there anybody at school you did get on with?

Gemma: Friends or teachers?

Interviewer: Teachers and any adults.

Gemma: Miss Smith. Miss Guest at first, Linda, there was a few people, but there were teachers I knew I could wind up. Like Miss Selman; she was the head of the year. I would get on with her sometimes and then sometimes I'd know that if I said the wrong thing to her I would get suspended, so she was the person I would say something to, knowing I would get suspended or put into the unit, whatever.

Interviewer: So what happened from Year 11 onwards? Tell me about what happened then.

Gemma: I wor there much after the end of Year 10. I never really went, did I? I got expelled in the end; say, three quarters, no, about halfway through Year 10 I got expelled and then I was allowed to go back so many hours a day or so many hours a week and then I used to go at first but then stopped going completely as I day have to. So I stopped doing it. But I did go in halfway through Year 10. I went to work at a primary school for a bit and then I just couldn't be bothered to go any more so I stopped doing that as well.

Interviewer: So what happened when the end of Year 11 came? What did you do then?

Gemma: How old was I then, 16? When I was 16 I got pregnant with him, day I? So after I left school, near enough straight away I got pregnant with the baby and I was at David's mom's. I was 17 in July and had him in October. So after school I had the baby.

Interviewer: So have you done any sort of work or training or anything since?

Gemma: I went to J Training down W for a bit.

Interviewer: And what sort of things did you do there?

Gemma: Just, like, Maths and English and stuff like that. I used to have to go to Connexions every week as well 'cause I was on benefits and to get my benefits I had to go to Connexions once every month so I could get paid. So I did that for a couple of months until I had the baby and then I stopped going after that.

Interviewer: And, so, was it Linda that you saw at Connexions when you went?

Gemma: And Fiona.

Interviewer: And how did you get on with those?

Gemma: Fine. Linda, like, I've got on with Linda from when I was at school, so I knew she worked at W some days of the week so we just used to purposely ask for her and after a couple of months when she worked more at the school than she did at W, then I got to know Fiona. So I used to see Fiona if Linda weren't there or see both of them.

Interviewer: So what sort of help did they give you?

Gemma: They, like, Linda got me into J Training I think and they used to phone me up and say there were, like, open events, blah blah blah, will you attend mother and baby classes? They did use to try and get me to college and I used to say I'd go but then I never used to turn up for it.

Interviewer: So looking back, then, if you knew now, if you could go back, would you do anything different?

Gemma: Yeah, I wish – if I could go back, if I could turn back time, I wish that I'd be able to sit down like I am with you now with teachers, so I know that things would be different, do you know what I mean. If I had, like, could just sit in a room with a couple of teachers and speak to them, things would have been different but I just wouldn't ever sit down, nothing like that, do you know what I mean.

Interviewer: How different do you think it would be? What sort of things do you think would be different?

Gemma: Then maybe I would have took my exams, do you know what I mean. Even, like, not taking my exams was just showing off really; I just day do it cause I thought I would be the only one that day do it. Do you know what I mean. But I wish I would have done it now. If I could go back I would have sat down and listened to people.

Interviewer: Right, Gemma, just one last question. How did things change when you had Dylan?

Gemma: I was all right with Mom anyway; I never really fell out with my mom – it was just when she tried to tell me to do this, and do that. When

I first told her I was pregnant with Dylan, obviously she day like it and we did fall out at first and I day speak to her for, say, the first six months. Then once she realized I wor,[3] that I was going to keep him and that I wor going to get rid of him or anything, she was fine with it, do you know what I mean, and learnt to live with it. It was going to happen anyway. Anyway I had a lot of support from David's mom and dad so I was fine. But everything was fine and that then.

Interviewer: How do you think having Dylan has changed you?

Gemma: It's made me a lot better – I can actually go out now and go clubbing with my mates down W or B and come back home to the baby. If I day have him I'd go to W fighting, not being bothered, getting that drunk I don't know where I am, stuff like that, do you know what I mean. I have changed a lot, like; I'm a lot more grown up now. Having Dylan just made me grow up. Same for David as well; it made him have to grow up.

Interviewer: So, Gemma, we were just talking a little there about when you were younger and you had gone through some things that you think impacted on school. Can you just tell me a little bit about those?

Gemma: Yep, when I was younger before I got pregnant, there was always a lot of going to solicitors, being recorded for this, that and the other to use at court 'cause my mom and nan were at court together and that. I've always had to be grown up and explain to Sarah, and my other younger sister Charlotte, like, what was going on and stuff like that. So when I was at school that was the only time I really got to be a kid; like, mess around and do stuff that I wanted to do 'cause when I was at home I had to be grown-up.

Interviewer: Were the school aware of that?

Gemma: They was. I think they did know what had gone on 'cause, like, they used to have to send my nan my school reports and stuff 'cause she used to ask for it, 'cause my dad wasn't allowed anything to do with us and stuff like that. So they was aware; but I think – no one ever asked me about it at school or nothing like that.

Interviewer: OK, that's great. Thank you, Gemma.

Gemma's mother's story

Interviewer: So, tell me a little about Gemma and school and how that went.

Mother: I don't know much about junior, what do they call it – primary school but I wasn't, well, I was around but, I don't know, I was naughty as a kid as well growing up and I lost them for five years and then I had them back.

Interviewer: Yes.

---

[3] wasn't

Mother: And I think she had a couple of weeks left in her primary school and then she went to M in Year 7. Things was good in Year 7 up until, I'd say, about ten months into it. After about ten months into it Gemma changed; not nastiness, not like, changed to a nasty person. I don't know what it was; I think it was the wrong crowd. She started dossing with the wrong crowd and...

Interviewer: And it kind of got her into trouble a bit?

Mother: She would always get the blame wherever; even if it weren't Gemma, Gemma would get the blame. So whatever happened, it was always Gemma's fault. Half the time – well, near enough every day – I'd be down the school for something. Gemma would be in trouble and I'd have to walk down the school being pregnant with the littleun[15]. The next day it would happen again, back down the school again, wor it. She didn't like school, that's all.

Interviewer: How did you get on with the school?

Mother: Not very good. I got on with Miss Ashton, Miss Claire and Mr Harris. I weren't too keen on Mr Goddard.

Interviewer: So there were some issues at school.

Mother: With Gemma, yeah. Fire alarms was one of them, I think. I remember the fire alarm and they were going to charge us for the fire alarms. And then she admitted doing it the second time, not the first time.

Interviewer: So how did things change, then, towards the end of secondary school? What happened with Gemma then?

Mother: Things changed a lot. I'd only just had them back, 'cause I lost them for five years, so when I did get her and Sarah back and they went to high school, I didn't want to send them. I'd say to them: well, "Don't go to school if you don't feel like it, you ain't got to go," 'cause I hadn't spent no time with them, so I wanted to spend my time with them and catch up on the five years I'd missed out on, like. So I used to say, "If you don't want to go to school, you know we'll go shopping or something." I think me losing her; me losing her had an impact on school in a way, I think.

Interviewer: So did that change towards Years 10 and 11?

Mother: Yes, 'cause I used to make them go to school from, from 18 months, beginning of Year 9, I think. I used to make them go to school and make her wear her uniform. Then she'd put her trainers in her bag and then I'd get a phone call; her ain't wearing the correct uniform. I sent her in her uniform; she'd go in jeans and a T-shirt and trainers – things she knew she weren't allowed to go in. She'd stop listening to what I'd say, we'd start bickering and then she moved out and moved in with David's mom and dad.

Interviewer: And when was that?

Mother: I think that was at the end of Year 9. Yeah, towards the end of Year 9. She only moved two doors away.

Interviewer: OK.

Mother: So I'd still get to see her every day, but I got – well, when Gemma didn't go to school, I don't know what she was doing round there but I got a fine; I had a fine for her for not going to school.

Interviewer: OK.

Mother: I had to pay a fine; I had to pay the fine in the end.

Interviewer: OK. And so how did things develop with David?

Mother: Ah, David's all right; they had their ups and downs like every couple but now; then he was cheeky – a little sod he was – but now he's had to grow up, like; he's got a babby[4] and has had to grow up a lot.

Interviewer: What happened when Gemma fell pregnant, then? How was it at that time?

Mother: It was a shock at first. Because I said to her, you know, I says, "Is this what you really want, a baby?" because I looked at her and Gemma looks so much like me, the things she's done; everything I have done, she's done and I says to her I didn't want – at first I didn't want her to have him, 'cause it's my life repeating over again, you know, so I says to her, "Have a sit down and have a good think about it you know, you're only young, you can get a good job," and, um, she refused and said it was her body, her baby and she was keeping him, so; then we ended up with him, dain't[5] we, yeah, and he's naughty, ay, he. But I think having him has changed her a lot, because she has always been grown up but she has grown up, a hell of a lot.

Interviewer: And so that was…When did she have Dylan?

Mother: I think she had him when she left school; after she'd left school.

Interviewer: OK, and so…

Mother: She turned 17 and she had him in the October.

Interviewer: And so she didn't do anything. She didn't get a job or do any training?

Mother: She used to go to Connexions.

Interviewer: Yeah.

Mother: I don't think she wanted to work. She went to Connexions and I thought, she thinks that having a baby at such an early time in life she didn't need to work 'cause that's what young moms think, you know: I'll have a baby and I ain't got to work and all this. So that's what I think she thinks.

Interviewer: How do you feel about that?

---

[4] baby
[5] didn't

[Pause.]

Interviewer: What would you like for her?

Mother: We've just got him into a playgroup now, so I'm hoping now when this one comes and it's like the same age as him, they can both be in a job, she can go [pause]. I don't mind having them but he's a handful, he is, terrible.

Interviewer: But you'd be there to support?

Mother: Yeah. He'd be at full-time school so I wouldn't mind.

Interviewer: How different do you think things would be if school was different or the situation was different?

Mother: If she didn't have kids or... I think if she didn't have Dylan; I think if she had stopped at school and carried on with her football training, her football skills – she's ever so good at sports and football. She was playing for W football team – so I think if she hadn't got pregnant with Dylan she would have carried on with her football career and had a career in football or something, sports or something like that if she hadn't had the babby.

Interviewer: Is that something she may return to?

Mother: I don't think so, no. She'll still play football but no; no chance now. She shows David up and he wouldn't have that.

School's story – Pastoral Head

Interviewer: OK, so we're here today, then, to talk about Gemma.

Pastoral Head: Yep.

Interviewer: Can you just describe Gemma for me from your point of view.

Pastoral Head: When Gemma started the school, she was a very angry child, um, didn't like authority, had no actual love, she had no love, no compassion, no empathy and she was against everything and everybody; anybody that had got a little bit more than her or spoke differently to her or challenged her, she didn't like it. So, but now, I do believe she has matured into a nice young lady.

Interviewer: How did you work with Gemma when she was at the school?

Pastoral Head: First of all I came across Gemma – the first time I actually came across Gemma was when she was in Year 8 and I asked her to put a tie on and she said no and I says, "No, you have to put a tie on," and she says, "If you ask me once more, me mom will come down and smack you one." So that was my first encounter with Gemma. And so I did say to her that, "No, I'm not frightened of your mom and your mom can come to the school at any time and meet with me but I'll stand here until you put your tie on."

Interviewer: How did she react to that?

Pastoral Head: She wasn't very impressed; she stood there. She was never an aggressive child but she used to challenge; every time you challenged her, she'd come back with a counter challenge and she did hide behind her mom a lot of the time. She used her mom to frighten people, to say her mom would come in and you'd never met her mom; but at the time she did put her tie on, but she did say to me that my mom would be coming down to school to see me.

Interviewer: So what were things like at home for Gemma?

Pastoral Head: When I got to know Gemma better like, I did find out that Mom had had her at a very early age; she was 14 when she actually had her; she had been in prison for GBH, which Gemma did tell me on several occasions, "My mom's bin done for hitting somebody. My mom has also been into a school and hit a teacher." She did tell me she had attacked a teacher – she was quite open about that – and she…I think sometimes she used that as a weapon against teachers to sort of scare them. Gemma was not violent herself, she wasn't a fighter. If she did have a fight with anyone it was always – it was very, very rare; it was more that Gemma used her mouth and threatened as opposed to being physical, but if she did, it never lasted very long because Mom was always there. Mom was always aware of Gemma having this fight, so it was like Gemma hid behind Mom and everything that Mom did. Gemma was trying, in a way, to emulate Mom because that is the only way she knew how to deal with things. Everything that Gemma said and when you met Mom, Gemma was, like, saying exactly what Mom was saying and she was emulating her mom, whereas when I started to work with her she didn't want me sitting by her so I deliberately sat by her. And she protested and protested to the point where she used to get up out of her classes and walk out because I was sitting next to her. But then I would follow her and it was like, "You're not going to win. I will be here, I will be supporting you and you will have no choice in this. I obviously know what's best."

But I did get a good relationship with her; I did speak to her about it and what I started to do was not, how can I say it, not to actually run Mom down or anything as she believed in Mom, but tried to, to twist the way she was thinking. Try to let her see how people would perceive Mom as violent, and, can I say, bad mouthed. She was always swearing and things like this. I tried to give her a little bit to empower her to look at other people's points of view, where they were coming from. But first of all she never liked me; she never ever liked me but then I did get inside and I did keep saying, and the more I kept saying to her, "You're a nice girl and if you smile…" – I think she just used to smile because she was fed up of me saying it, to be honest. And I used to say, "You're a really nice girl, you should show people that you are a nice girl." And that way I sort of got inside her hard core exterior.

Interviewer: How did things develop throughout school? So as she went up the years, how did she develop?

Pastoral Head: She started looking at – she started empathizing with teachers. She started looking at it from their point of view, obviously realizing they hadn't got the backgrounds that she got – and then she started turning and was more angry towards Mom for the way she behaved; and she did start saying to me that she was embarrassed about Mom coming to school and she didn't want Mom there. She asked me to go to meetings. If there were any meetings to do with her behaviour or anything like that, she preferred me to be there rather than Mom. Which, in a way, was – can I say, it made me feel proud that she was actually changing but obviously I still had to keep Mom in the picture because I also wanted Mom to be part of this change because Gemma had got younger siblings and she had got young brothers and sisters, and I thought if you don't change Mom's outlook on school, then you're not going to change Gemma's. In the long run it's just going to have a knock-on effect and the next child is going to be brought up and think they can get away with everything at school. So I did try to include Mom and kept saying to Gemma, well, I'll be there, but your mom should be there as well. And I did build up a relationship with Mom so later on in the school it was more that Gemma was talking to teachers, smiling at teachers and wearing correct uniform. She wasn't a golden child; she wasn't perfect, she wasn't. Gemma was Gemma: a lovely child – she even had the headteacher saying how nice she was; you know, that she was a good child. She was always open and honest – she never lied, she told you exactly what she'd done but she wouldn't sometimes tell you who the people with her were as she didn't want to be known as a grass or anything like that. But she would tell me and then I'd go about it in a different way.

Interviewer: How about her attendance at school, what was that like?

Pastoral Head: It was really bad to start with; she wouldn't come into school and Mom very rarely rang in. We used to have to ring Mom, but I found out later it was because Mom had no money to put credit on her phone to ring the school. So obviously we used to ring Mom, but later on, I should say more so at the end of Year 10, she wanted to come in to school because she felt that this was where she belonged and she felt she got more respect, more love or whatever from school than she did at home; so she didn't want to spend time with Mom, she wanted to be in school.

Interviewer: If you had to describe her motivation of where she was going and what she wanted to do in the future, how would you describe that?

Pastoral Head: When she was younger, she had no motivation at all; there was no purpose, she had no purpose in life. There was no reason for her to learn; there was no reason for her to come to school. Pointless, didn't want to be here, wanted to be at home. Later on when she was aware of what she could gain with her results and different things and the jobs she could do, you know, working with us, not just me but my colleagues as well, she found that she had got more potential and she'd be able to go out there and find a job – so, yes, she had got more motivation later on. She was getting down to her coursework and she was staying with us and doing her coursework. She found it difficult at home, obviously, because of her siblings and because of Mom's attitude that she would rather babysit than be doing homework – so, yes, she was motivated before she left.

Interviewer: OK. And then during Year 11 things changed quite a bit for Gemma. How do you think the issues that she went through there – how do you think that affected her?

Pastoral Head: Well, if you're talking about school issues, they asked for her to be permanently excluded due to the fire alarm incident. Yeah, that was just a silly – all it was was that Gemma lifted the plastic for another lad to hit. That's what she told me, but she didn't say that to the others. She wanted to take the full responsibility because she lifted the plastic. I did fight for her. She was disappointed with herself; totally and completely disappointed. We both were and she knows that I had major feelings for her; motherly feelings towards her, protective feelings towards her, so she knew she had disappointed me. She was deeply upset and she realized she'd done wrong but going back over the years she couldn't see why this incident would get her a permanent exclusion whereas the incidents prior to that, which were more severe, wouldn't, but I just says that it was an ongoing thing and this was just the icing on the cake.

Interviewer: So which part of the year did this happen?

Pastoral Head: Well, she was able to return afterwards but they said she could only return under my guidance. And she had to sit with me all day, completing her coursework. She wasn't allowed on site or anywhere else, 'cause I fought hard for her. Well, we all did really. But we said that she could do something with herself if she continued but then I do believe at the end of Year 11 she got in with a lad, which is understandable, and I think some of the influences from him sort of persuaded her not to come as often as she could. If she hadn't been with him at the time, she would have come in and completed all of her coursework. Which I was disappointed about after, but then I thought, well, I've done what I can, do you know what I mean. But then she got in with a lad and wouldn't come to school that often because he didn't come to school. He had already been permanently excluded.

Interviewer: If you could change any of the influences around Gemma or her situation, do you think that would have made a difference?

Pastoral Head: I think it would have made a difference if I had picked her up in Year 7 – or even in primary school – and worked with her slowly; and obviously her age – as she matures it makes a difference; they start taking responsibility. But, Gemma apparently in primary school, sat down many a time and hid behind this image of her mother and that she would come to school and she would do this and that. She did want to emulate her mom. It weren't till later on that she realized that it wasn't the way that Mom should be; it was her way, you know and there was a way to change. She did go and live with Nan for some time and I think that was Dad's mom. No, it was mom's Mom. She went to live there for a time because she didn't want to live at home. And Nan – absolutely brilliant while she was living with Nan.

Interviewer: Did she ever live anywhere else?

Pastoral Head: Not that I know of. There was a couple of times where she stayed at her boyfriend's. And his family was a strong family compared to – there was Mom and Dad and sisters and they have been an influence on her. And Mom wasn't a bad influence and neither were her sisters because they introduced her to holidays abroad and life, you know – life with cars and that. It was just, and I do know about that, but that wasn't a bad influence at all and so I wasn't really concerned about that. But I know she only stayed there because he lived down the road and she'd stay there a couple of nights and then she would go back home when she fell out with Mom.

Interviewer: How was her written work? What were her basic skills like?

Pastoral Head: Very capable, very capable. Understanding skills, very capable. Maths wasn't one of her strongest subjects. English was probably one of her best, like, well, one of her better subjects. Maths wasn't one of her strongest subjects and obviously she didn't see the point in maths in Year 7, well, 8 and 9. But as she moved on she realized that it was valuable.

Interviewer: Anything else that you remember about Gemma? Or anything else that may be relevant?

Pastoral Head: No, very stubborn child; early days, very stubborn. Still stubborn today, but can see, willing to back down, previously she wasn't willing to back down – there was no alternative to Gemma: it was her way or no way. Now she has taken on board that there is another way and, you know, just listen to people – and she will listen to opinions and I think she has done well for herself and has got two children.

Interviewer: Did that happen around school time?

Pastoral Head: No, it was when she left school. She fell in love – she fell in love in Year 9. We knew about her love for this lad and when he actually, she was happy with him in Year 11. I did speak to him as well and I said, "You know, both of you can make a future for yourselves, but you've both got to try hard. If that's the way you want to be you've got to start doing things and whatever," and I did speak to him as well as Gemma. I says, "Please don't stop her coming into school. Let her come into school and get her grades and things." And he was fine – I had a good relationship. But she loved him from Year 9 so you knew that once she had set up a relationship with him in Year 11, it was like, well, that's it now, she's got what she wanted, but yeah.

Interviewer: Well, that's great. Thanks very much for your time.

David's story (boyfriend)

Interviewer: OK, so we're here, then, to talk about Gemma and Gemma's time at school from your point of view really. So tell me a little bit about how and when you met Gemma.

David: When I met her at first she was at primary school. She moved round the estate. And then, like, I don't know, then we just ended up going to M with each other and, like, I don't know, it was, like, mad. 'Cause, like, we were both naughty at school ay it really and then – I don't really know how to explain her.

Interviewer: What sort of things did you get up to that made you naughty?

David: Like, wagging school and that, smoking when we weren't supposed to be smoking and stuff like that. And then she used to set all the fire alarms off and stuff like that really.

Interviewer: Was that from the start? Or how was it from the start?

David: At the start it was all right 'cause like, Year 7 and that, everyone dain't know each other and that and then when we all started making mates with everyone, that's when it all used to get, like, worser, you know what I mean.

Interviewer: So when did that start happening?

David: I'd say Year 9 or summat;[6] about Year 9 I think.

Interviewer: OK. So the general stuff you got up to kind of kicked off in Year 9. Any incident in particular you can remember?

---

[6] something

David: I ain't sure, really.

Interviewer: Ok. Did you tend to get into trouble with the teachers a lot, then?

David: Yeah.

Interviewer: When did you start going out with Gemma?

David: Uh, I think it was Year 11, I think. I used to go out with her before that, then when we properly got together it was Year 11.

Interviewer: OK. And so when you were in Year 11, what was Gemma like at school? What was she like with her work?

David: She was all right, she's, like, clever and that but it's like, 'cause when; I think when she was doing her, what's it called now, work in a nursery and that, like, when she was doing all that stuff and that, she was doing all right with it. But, and then she just packed it in for some reason. Like, she talks about it now – like she wishes she could still, like, go back to school and that and do all her GCSEs and that.

Interviewer: So how was her attendance?

David: It was – I reckon it was good but it depends; like, some days she'd be like, she wouldn't care and some days she'd, like, get on with her work and that.

Interviewer: OK, so it was a bit hit and miss.

David: Yeah, she just had them odd days.

Interviewer: What would you say about her motivation?

David: Uh, I don't know.

Interviewer: Did she want to go to school?

David: Yeah, I think she did want to go to school but, dunno – it was just one of those things.

Interviewer: What about family? What about the situation with family?

David: Uh, it was all right, I think. It was, like, 'cause, like, Sarah used to go to school with us and Gemma used to walk to school with Sarah and then Charlotte used to go to H Junior School.

Interviewer: Were they sisters?

David: Yeah, all three sisters, yeah.

Interviewer: And how about Mom?

David: She used to stay at home.

Interviewer: What about the situation sort of more towards Year 11? How were things then, 'cause I know there was some sort of movement then with where she lived round about then?

David: It was, like – 'cause she, like, used to live with her mom and then; then I think they had a, like, big bust up and then she moved in with me, like.

Interviewer: And when was that?

David: Um, it was in Year 11. I cor remember what month or what.

Interviewer: OK, so in Year 11, Gemma came to stay with you and your family?

David: Yeah.

Interviewer: So who was in the house? Who was your family?

David: There was me, my mom, Gemma – there was my two brothers and my sister.

Interviewer: And how did Gemma get on living with you guys?

David: At first she was nervous, she day speak to no one and then after a bit, like – she's like a sister to everyone now, like, with my brother and all of 'um.

Interviewer: OK. And then Gemma became pregnant.

David: Yeah.

Interviewer: And when was that?

David: Um, when did she have Dylan, 19 October 2010, I think.

Interviewer: How were things then?

David: It was all right, it was just, like; when she had Dylan, it was just really cramped, so my brother's upstairs, and my other brother's upstairs and so the two bedrooms was full upstairs and my mom and dad had their own room. My sister had to sleep on the settee and we had to have the back room. So it was all cramped…

Interviewer: So it was all cramped…

David: And then we ended up getting this house.

Interviewer: So how was it – was Gemma pregnant at school?

David: Nah.

Interviewer: So was it at school or after?

David: After school.

Interviewer: So how were things when she left school?

David: Um.

Interviewer: What did she do when she left school?

David: I think she did do something – I know she worked in a pub for a little bit, cleaning and that. Um, I ay[7] sure what else she done. Think she did some other things, though. Think she went to college as well.

Interviewer: For a little while?

David: Yeah. That was when she was pregnant with Dylan.

Interviewer: OK.

David: Then she stopped.

---

[7] I'm not

Interviewer: So how were things after Dylan?

David: It was all right, yeah, it was a bit mad.

Interviewer: I'm sure. So how were things with you when you left school?

David: Me, um, it was all right like, 'cause when I left school, I went to college. I think I done, like, a year at college and then, like, after, I left like because Gemma was pregnant with Dylan.

Interviewer: And I hear you had some good news this morning?

David: Yeah, someone phoned for a job so I'm going to work today to have an interview.

Interviewer: Fantastic, brilliant. OK, so one last question. If you had to describe Gemma when she was at school, how would you describe her?

David: Um, when she wor[8] with her mates she was good; she'd get on with her work and everything, so – I don't know how to describe her really; just one of them, like.

Interviewer: OK that's brilliant – thanks ever so much for your time.

David: That's all right.

Connexions personal adviser's story (Linda)

Interviewer: So tell me a little bit about the first time you met Gemma.

Connexions: The first time I met Gemma she was brought into me by the head of year and Gemma came in with a very stand-offish attitude; didn't want to be there, didn't want me to talk to her, didn't want any part of it – and it was a case of breaking down barriers very, very gently with Gemma and once she realized that she could trust, she became very relaxed and very comfortable and it did take, not that long really, but we did get there and I engaged with Gemma very, very well.

Interviewer: OK. So tell me a little bit about how she was at school.

Connexions: Gemma hated school, hated every part of school, hated the teachers, just didn't get on there and didn't want to be there. She didn't want any part of the lessons during Year 11; end of Year 10, 11, she wasn't in any lessons, she didn't go to any lessons.

Interviewer: So her attendance would have been quite poor?

Connexions: Yeah, absolutely. We got to a stage towards the end of Year 10/beginning of Year 11 where her attendance started to get better; she was starting to come and then middle of Year 11 to the end of Year 11, she didn't see the point. She didn't see the point of being there so she didn't bother to turn up.

---

[8] was

Interviewer: OK. How would you say things were at home at the time? Were you aware of what was happening at the time?

Connexions: Yeah, I mean, I suppose to a certain degree. Gemma's mom and her relationship became, um; it broke down slightly because Mom was starting to lay the law down because Mom was receiving phone calls and having trouble from school due to Gemma's poor attendance. So Mom started to lay the law down and Gemma didn't like it. Gemma had got away with it for so long and it was a case of, well, you know, I'm not going to put up with this anymore, kind of thing, and she didn't like it so the relationship at home broke down slightly.

Interviewer: Did this affect where she then lived?

Connexions: Yes – she actually moved in with her boyfriend's parents.

Interviewer: How was Gemma's behaviour?

Connexions: Gemma was fine if she got on with you. But if she didn't get on with you, then that was it, basically. She was absolutely fine, I didn't have a problem with Gemma in any way, shape or form. She didn't cause me any grief, she wasn't discourteous to me, she wasn't rude to me; I didn't have a problem with Gemma. There was a couple of other members of staff that didn't have a problem with Gemma, but on the whole, she didn't get on with them. Gemma had gained this reputation early on in her schooling and she felt that she had to live up to it.

Interviewer: How would you say Gemma's motivation was at school?

Connexions: She didn't have any. She had no motivation at all because she didn't see the point in it, she hated it, she didn't see the point in it, so there was no motivation there for her. She was in the behaviour unit in G-Block most of the time – or all of the time, really. But she didn't do a lot in there. She didn't cause any grief in there, but she didn't do a lot in there either. She just, you know; when she was in school, she would go to G-Block and that was where she stayed for the whole of the day. She didn't, you know; she didn't cause any grief in there because she got along with the people that were running G-Block so she was fine in G-Block. But if they tried to integrate her back into lessons, it didn't work.

Interviewer: So did you work with Gemma when she left school?

Connexions: Yes, I worked with Gemma throughout Year 11, very early in Year 11 and towards the end of Year 10, really, but more intensely in Year 11 and afterwards.

Interviewer: OK, and so what sort of support did you give Gemma towards the end of Year 11 and when things started to change?

Connexions: I was trying to get her to engage in something and Gemma didn't want to engage in anything and we would arrange numerous appointments and she just didn't go; and then Gemma found out she was pregnant and she had a little baby boy and we tried to get her involved in the young moms-to-be programmes and young parenting programmes and all kinds of things and Gemma would always say, "Yeah, yeah I'll go," but she never, ever went. Never.

Interviewer: Did she do or start anything?

Connexions: She started at J Training for a very short period of time but it was only a very short period of time and then she just didn't go and that was it. And then we never really got her engaged in anything after that, kind of thing, that was it.

Interviewer: And how do you think things could have been different? Is there anything you can think of at school or afterwards that could have changed?

Connexions: At the time, when Gemma was going through this situation, I think very little would have changed because that was the way Gemma was at that time. Looking at Gemma today, Gemma has grown up dramatically; she's a parent and she has grown up. I think if Gemma could change things then maybe she would. But at the time, that was Gemma and you weren't going to change her; nothing was going to change her. She was strong, she was very strong willed, she was very strong minded, she knew what she wanted to do and it was very difficult to deter her from it.

Interviewer: If you had to describe Gemma as a person then?

Connexions: Then? To me?

Interviewer: Yes, to you.

Connexions: Gemma was, as I said to you, was well-mannered, courteous, kind, polite, she would engage, she would sit and talk, she would moan at me, she would groan at me, she would, but none of it in a vicious way, none of it in a nasty way. That was Gemma. To staff at school Gemma was a living nightmare because that was the reputation she had got and Gemma had got to live up to that reputation.

Interviewer: Do you think that reputation was true?

Connexions: No, that wasn't the real Gemma; that was a front.

Analysis of citations:

Unstable accommodation	1
Low motivation	7
Unemployment in family	2
Poor behaviour in school	2
Poor school attendance	16

Chapter 8

Wayne

Wayne is white, speaks English as his first language and was raised by his birth mother who is now living with a new partner. Wayne is living at home but spends a lot of time with Sue, the mother of his son, Kevin. Sue and Kevin live with Sue's mother in the area.

Wayne's risk factor score was 10, arising from:

Low basic skills
Low motivation
Unemployment in family
Poor behaviour in school
LDD (he was on the SEN Code of Practice)

Interviews were conducted with Wayne and his mother in their home. Wayne's family were present during the interviews. The second interviewer was a Connexions personal adviser, Jessica, who was known to the family. Interviews were also conducted with his Connexions personal adviser, Sarah, and the special educational needs coordinator (SENCo) of the school at the time. The learning support assistant, Jane, was also interviewed. The school has been named Woodbury for this text.

Timeline for Wayne

Date	Activity
Statutory school leaving	Birth of Son Kevin
June 2008	NEET
July 2008	
Aug 2008	
Sept 2008	
Oct 2008	Nacro
Nov 2008	
Dec 2008	
Jan 2009	
Feb 2009	
March 2009	
April 2009	
May 2009	NEET
June 2009	Nacro
July 2009	Age UK
Aug 2009	NEET
Sept 2009	
Oct 2009	
Nov 2009	Argos
Dec 2009	
Jan 2010	
Feb 2010	NEET
March 2010	

April 2010	
May 2010	
June 2010	Logistics apprentice
July 2010	
Aug 2010	
Sept 2010	
Oct 2010 – to date	Groundworks crew member

Wayne's story

Interviewer: Good. We're here to talk about the times when you leave school and you are not in education, employment, or training. What I want you to do is to tell me about your time at Woodbury, the secondary school, to start with. Bear in mind that your mum is here and she has told me about your time there. What was secondary school like? What can you remember about it?

Wayne: Um. Never used to do good in there.

Interviewer: Right.

Wayne: Getting kicked out.

Interviewer: Right. Do you remember any staff you liked who seemed to like you?

Wayne: Mr Brington.

Interviewer: OK. What was his role? What did he teach?

Wayne: English.

Interviewer: OK, and you got on OK with him?

Wayne: Yeah.

Interviewer: Were there any staff that you really didn't get on with?

Wayne: My head of year sometimes.

Interviewer: Yes. Who was that?

Wayne: Mr Leighton.

Interviewer: I don't know any of these staff. When you started at school your mom said that it was sort of OK. It was all right. It kind of got worse the further up the school you went.

Wayne: Yeah, that's right.

Interviewer: Can you tell us a bit more about that? Can you remember what made life more difficult?

Wayne: Um, I ain't quite sure. I think it was because I became violent to staff or summat.

Interviewer: What can you remember about that?

Wayne: They just kicked me out and I had to come back after school for lessons.

Interviewer: Can you remember a typical incident? Something you kicked off at?

Wayne: I cor remember.

Interviewer: Was it in Year 10 or 11 that you became a dad?

Wayne: Year 11.

Interviewer: OK. And what happened when you left school? What did you do?

Wayne: I went to N Training.

Interviewer: And that was after you left school, was it?

Wayne: Yes.

Interviewer: How long were you at N Training?

Wayne: Well, I done manufacturing, then I went on to mechanics, and I got nothing in them both.

Interviewer: You got nothing?

Wayne: No.

Interviewer: So that doesn't sound like it was that good.

Wayne: No. It wor no good.

Interviewer: And what happened after that?

Wayne: I went to Age Concern.

Interviewer: Age Concern?

Wayne: Yeah.

Interviewer: OK. What did you do there?

Wayne: Nothing. I just got my maths and English, that's all. I ain't got courses no more.

Interviewer: And all of this was after you left school. Were you still in Year 11 when this happened or was this, like, much later than that?

Wayne: Later than that, but I did do work experience.

Interviewer: So what sort of work experience did you do?

Wayne: Mechanics.

Interviewer: Was that before N Training?

Wayne: Before.

Interviewer: So it was Woodbury, N Training, Age Concern, then what?

Wayne: Argos. Yeah, Argos. Delivery assistant.

Interviewer: What happened then?

Wayne: That was only over Christmas.

Interviewer: Which Christmas was it?

Wayne: It wor two Christmases ago.

Interviewer: So how long were you there?

Wayne: I think I was about 17 or 16.

Interviewer: So after Argos what happened then?

Wayne: Um, I got an apprenticeship as a van driver.

Interviewer: And now?

Wayne: I got all my certificates. NVQs, carrying and delivering goods level 2, um, van driver.

Interviewer: That's good. And so what are you doing now?

Wayne: I'm working with Groundworks. Maintaining the canals and, like, building steps and, like, just cleaning the area. Good pay.

Interviewer: It always helps, doesn't it? And how long does that go on for?

Wayne: Two more months.

Interviewer: OK, and then what?

Wayne: Um, they might be offering permanent jobs out on the land team. So it's just, like, doing the cracks up and that. Building stuff on them.

Interviewer: Have there been times when you haven't had an apprenticeship or a job or a college? What did you do then?

Wayne: Go on the dole.

Interviewer: And how do you spend your days?

Wayne: Go down Sue's house.

Interviewer: So have they been for long periods of time out of work?

Wayne: No, not long.

Interviewer: So you have been in and out of work?

Wayne: Yeah.

Interviewer: If there was one thing about school that you could change what would it be?

Wayne: Behave more.

Interviewer: All right. Anything about the training places, the N Training, the Age Concern, that lot?

Wayne: Well, I would have tried harder, but they weren't giving, like, enough respect to anyone, to be fair.

Interviewer: So how was that shown? How did they not show respect?

Wayne: They hardly learn you nothing.

Interviewer: But it sounds like you're doing OK at the Groundworks place and the van driving seems to have been a positive experience.

Wayne: Yeah.

Jessica: Can I just ask about Sue and Kevin? How was that at school, because that would have happened right at the end? Was Sue at school with you?

Wayne: Yep.

Interviewer: So how did that affect things? Being at school when all of that was happening?

Wayne: It didn't affect nothing. Just how she went to Batman's Hill and done all her stuff there.

Interviewer: And what about visiting your son? I know that you go a lot and that you went a lot when you were at school. How did you manage to fit all that in with your work and your training?

Wayne: I found a way [laughs]. I went every day.

Interviewer: So you were quite committed to go and help.

Wayne: Yeah.

Interviewer: I think that is about it. Is there anything you would like to ask me or Jessica?

Wayne: [Shakes head.]

Jessica: Just one more question. You know when you left school, you didn't do exams.

Wayne: I did do some of them, but I failed on them.

Interviewer: OK. And so then did you work with Connexions to get N Training sorted?

Wayne: Yeah, I did.

Interviewer: So that bit when you left was like trying to figure out what to do and where to go?

Wayne: Sarah helped me do all that.

Interviewer: How did Sarah help you?

Wayne: Sarah just used to, like, if I day, like, look for training or a job and that, she would come down me ear hole. And she used to phone my mom up and, you know, when I had an interview, she'd phone about two hours before, even if it wor 7 o'clock in the morning. She phoned me or my mom up.

Interviewer: Yeah, what did she say?

Wayne: Just reminded me, make sure I go.

Interviewer: Yeah, did it help?

Wayne: Yeah.

Interviewer: Just out of interest, if they hadn't phoned, do you think you would have gone?

Wayne: Probably still be in bed if my mom day wake me up. 'Cause I'm a heavy sleeper.

Interviewer: I remember Sarah saying that you used to go down to see Kevin and then you used to help out and then go to your training and then come back and then help out...

Wayne: I'm always down there. Even though I've a job now.

Mother: We don't see him until it is time for bed.

Wayne's mother's story

Interviewer: Let's talk about Wayne. The reason we are talking about Wayne is that after he left school there was a period of time when he was not in education, employment, or training. To start with, just tell me about his secondary school experience. What did he say about his secondary school? Did he enjoy it? Was it difficult to get him to go? Did he get in trouble? What kind of stuff did he say?

Mother: He didn't enjoy it. He was in bottom class and I don't think they teached him much.

Interviewer: Often when some young people start secondary school it was all right, then they go downhill. Some people don't like it at all. What was Wayne like in junior school?

Mother: Lovely. Absolutely loved it.

Interviewer: So can you identify when he stopped liking school?

Mother: It was probably in his second year. When he was in his second year.

Interviewer: And can you identify anything in particular that he didn't like?

Mother: [Shakes head.]

Interviewer: That's OK. Is there anything that you can remember?

Mother: I think that the classes he was in; he couldn't really concentrate very well because the students used to run about.

Interviewer: Muck about?

Mother: Yeah.

Interviewer: When he got to the last two years at school, Years 10 and 11, how was his attendance? Did he go? Did he skive? What did he do?

Mother: I think he skived a couple of times, but they suspended him a couple of times as well.

Interviewer: Can you remember why?

Mother: One, they said he took a phone, but he never did and it wasn't proved. That was the one and the other one was because of a fight.

Interviewer: And so – I know that in his last year, I think his last year, he became a father.

Mother: Yeah, he did.

Interviewer: So how did that affect his schooling?

Mother: You know, it was OK. He just wanted to get out and get a job but he found it hard because he had no qualifications.

Interviewer: So let's talk about that bit now. You are allowed to leave school at the end of Year 11, when you are 16. What did he do then?

Mother: He went to, is it N Training college? That was the only college what he could get in. And they didn't really teach him that much and then he went back to Connexions and they helped him really good.

Interviewer: Tell me about N Training to start with.

Mother: I think it was English and maths I think he went for. And, you know, he did OK.

Jessica: Was it a bit too much like school?

Mother: Yeah.

Interviewer: Then he went off to Connexions. What happened? What did they do?

Mother: They found him, like, places, I mean; they helped him a lot, Connexions did.

Interviewer: So how long did that go on for? And what happened next?

Mother: Quite a few years [laughter], I think.

Mother: Yeah, quite a while.

Jessica: But he had some fantastic results.

Mother: Oh God, yes. He's come, he's come with certificates and all sorts. You know, he's got certificates for all the courses that he done with Connexions and that.

Interviewer: Oh good. What kind of courses were they?

Mother: I can't remember. You'll have to ask Wayne.

Interviewer: Has he had any jobs? I know we've talked about Argos. What kind of jobs?

Mother: Yes. He done the Argos over the Christmas period and he's done, he went for another placement I think he was driving, doing something with driving. And this one, it's, like, Groundworks. He likes this one, but it ends in April. He quite likes it; he likes to get out there and do it.

Interviewer: What's going to happen in April?

Mother: He's going to find it hard to find something else. Because the courses they've stopped, nearly everything now, really.

Interviewer: If you could change one thing about his time in school, what would it be?

Mother: I wish they hadn't chucked him out; I wish they'd kept him in the school and had somebody teaching him in a different classroom instead of chucking him out, because all they did when they was chucked out was go out instead of having to do work.

Interviewer: That's Wayne now. Let's stop.

The SENCo's story

Interviewer: You are aware that the purpose of this interview is to collect information about young people who have experienced not being in education, employment, or training – NEET?

SENCo: Yes.

Interviewer: The name that we are considering is Wayne and what I'd like you to do is start from the beginning and just tell me as far as you can the story of Wayne at Woodbury.

SENCo: He was obviously with us at the time when the school was called Woodbury. Wayne came to us, obviously, in Year 7 and I can't remember which primary school he came from, but when he came, I was the Special Needs Co-ordinator and I remained the Special Needs Co-ordinator all the time he was there. I also taught him maths for the majority of the years that he was there. So that's from Year 7 to Year 11. When Wayne first came to Woodbury, he, um there was a contradiction in how Wayne looked and how he actually performed. Uh, he had all the outward appearance of quite a bright young man: he had the glasses, he was very well attired and he looked, um, as if he would be in one of the top sets. But as it happened he did have problems with poor basic skills; his reading certainly wasn't what it should be, or spelling. Numeracy skills weren't great either. Um, I can't actually remember any figures. It would be helpful if I had access to records but I haven't.

Gradually, as Wayne worked through Year 7, Year 8, he to begin with was very eager to please. He wanted to do well, he was very co-operative and was a very good student in many ways. I believe that his attendance wasn't too bad at that time, but gradually as he went through the school system he became, you know; it was a classic case of, you know, uninterested and disaffected and gradually as he went through the school he never got to a point where behaviour became so bad or attainment became so bad that we had to move him from School Action to School Action Plus and get some funding for him, but he would certainly have been on the borderline of that case. He is one of the characters who, as we go through Key Stage 4 (Year 10, Year 11) became more and more disaffected, and he started to run with the big boys as far as behaviour was concerned. He got himself into scrapes and certainly within school. I'm not aware of anything like the youth offending team being involved, but I wouldn't be surprised if this was the case. Certainly, as well, when hormones kicked in and girls became apparent, it was evident that he would be so heavily involved with that. There were always running arguments and such going on within lessons between him and girls and gradually he became more disaffected and I believe that his attendance started to drop. I can't remember what actually happened towards the end of Year 11. He was one of these students who disappeared off the radar. Now if that is the time when he was becoming involved with Connexions and something outside school then I'm not absolutely sure, but this is going back three or four years now. It's difficult to remember everything, but that's as much, really, as I can remember. Is there any particular question that I can answer?

Interviewer: Given what we know now, that at the age of 17 he effectively dropped out – he didn't carry on with education, employment, or training – have you got any ideas about what that might have been about?

SENCo: Not really. As I said, he did show lots of, um, socializing problems as he got through. Whether they were issues of bullying I'm not sure. He was the sort of kid who might be victimized by some of the others, but he always actively stuck up for himself. He certainly wasn't a doormat and he would fight his corner and that, very often because he was being egged on by other kids; that would very often get him into trouble at school. There was one of our LSAs [learning support assistants] – who worked quite a lot with him, but, uh, on a day-to-day basis. He – he was a typical lower-end student who became gradually more disaffected as he went through the school. It's no surprise to me whatsoever that he didn't go into education, employment, or training when he left school and I would imagine that there wouldn't have been very much for him, um. I do know a little bit about the family background and I know, uh, his mother's family name and her family name were well known to us within the school and they had presented problems over the years and, um, there was no sort of, um, academic history within the family – no aspirations to do well either in education or particularly in employment and I would think that – I'm speaking totally off the top of my head – there wasn't much of a role model as far as people in employment or education was concerned.

Interviewer: I was going to ask you whether you would have been surprised to find that he didn't end up in education, employment, or training.

SENCo: Not surprised at all.

Interviewer: Is there anything you can remember about his relationship with other pupils? You mentioned possible bullying. Did he have a circle of friends?

SENCo: Yes, there were a few. But, uh, not sure whether they would be close friends or not, but there were certain similar type of kids that he did mix with, but, um, unfortunately, because of the sets he tended to be in, uh, there were also the kids who tended to take advantage and, uh. As I say, he always fought his corner, and very often he gave as good as he got, especially as he got older. And he got physically quite tall and, um, he was a kid who always seemed a bit uncomfortable in his skin to me. Yeah, as I said at the start, there was a contradiction: what you saw wasn't what you got. It was to begin with. He really tried hard. He was really sweet in Year 7 and Year 8, but gradually you could see the downward spiral. And, um, you know, there were instances of bad language and answering teachers back and that sort of thing. And some staff perhaps couldn't cope with him and he'd be sent to what was the time-out room at the time.

Interviewer: Is there anything else you would like to say?

SENCo: No, I would be interested to know exactly what happened to him and where he is now. If you see him, remember me to him and see if he remembers me as well.

Interviewer: Jessica has reminded you about something that has triggered a memory.

SENCo: Yes, it has triggered a memory. I do remember, did remember, mentioning about the hormones kicking in and he was particularly interested in girls and there was a, uh – an incident, well, more than an incident. In fact, when he was in Year 11 he was going out with a younger girl in the school and she, I believe, became pregnant. And, um, uh, obviously all the ensuing problems kicked in within school and that obviously led to his further disaffection. And I've just asked Jessica now whether he actually stayed to the end of Year 11 and we can't remember, but it would be interesting to, um, to find out if he actually did manage to do any exams or get anything at all. So…

Jessica: Don't think so.

SENCo: But, obviously, that was the sort of kid he was. As I say, he was, uh; he was always eager to please and he was, um, looking for friends, looking for affection a lot of the time and perhaps, uh, he found it [laughs].

Interviewer: Do you think that the incident with the girl had any impact on him dropping out of the system?

SENCo: Ah. Yes, probably, but it also did his street cred a lot of good while he was in Year 11 and he – for a while you could see him strutting around the place. Whether he understood the implications, at that point, of becoming a father – um, I don't think he probably did. But no doubt he has since found out.

Jane's story, learning support assistant, Woodbury School

Interviewer: So, we are talking about Wayne and just start by telling me when Wayne first came to the school.

Jane: Right, OK. Obviously I first met Wayne when he arrived in Year 7 and I used to support him in maths with Miss F. Wayne was a very innocent Year 7 young boy who, who tried his best at the time. Due to the teacher who was doing mathematics at the time, he was always quite well behaved and tried to do his best for him. So that would be the first recollection of Wayne at the time. I did support him again in Year 8. Same subject, maths – and I think I supported him sometimes in English as well. There'd be a difference from maths to English and I don't know whether that was due to the class teacher, to be honest.

Interviewer: Yes.

Jane: I sometimes found this with students, that you know, if they enjoyed something and got on with the teacher, they would excel. If they found things difficult and didn't like the teacher, obviously, that would be that case when there was no motivation, it was boring, and they didn't want to do the work, so I was obviously trying to support and motivate all the time. I can't remember supporting Wayne in Year 9, to be honest, but then I went on to support him in Year 10 and 11 but that was within English and his GCSE English coursework with Mr Brington. I saw a big difference in Wayne's change of motivation and when he wanted to work he would work but it was always a constant effort to encourage him to do this or he just didn't want to know. Whether that was part of the peer group that he was with at the time, I really couldn't say, but he was always with a group of lads and, you know, they was always the same group of lads that would be the same in the classroom as well who he would be with and even asking him to move would be a big issue because "why is it me?" and the usual remarks like that. Would you like me to mention that one incident?

Interviewer: Yes, yes.

Jane: OK, I do remember an incident with Wayne where this was in Year, I believe it was Year 10. When obviously I was trying to encourage Wayne to, to do some work and it was push the paper out the way and he didn't want to do it and, "Just leave me alone," type of thing and I actually remember him saying something quite derogatory. As a professional, I lost it, ha ha, and actually, you know, really went, went into his face about it. I know now, obviously, that that was wrong but he stood his ground and didn't back down; he was, like, in my face and I was in his face at the time and the teacher obviously intervened. I do remember him coming to apologize later whether it was the next session or what have you; yeah, I mean, that was just the sort of way things were that if Wayne really didn't want to do something there was no moving him, really no moving him. But when he knew he could do something and he wanted to do it, you know, he showed a good improvement in, well, he was; it was like Jekyll and Hyde, I suppose, in a sense that one minute he'd be fantastic and prove what he could really do and you would give him all the praise and he'd take all the praise on but when he didn't want to do it there was no motivating him whatsoever and that was it, he stood his ground, so...

Interviewer: That must have made things a little difficult.

Jane: Yes, it did. It did, but again, you know, I mean, obviously with certain circumstances. I don't know whether they are to do with family life or what have you, 'cause obviously we wasn't always told if anything was happening, you know, outside the family, and you do have to take these things into consideration when you're supporting and, you know, whether the low motivation comes from outside, within the school – you know, it's very hard to pinpoint sometimes.

Interviewer: Were you aware of anything that happened that would have affected Wayne?

Jane: No, not really. Again, I think it; within Wayne's peer group and Wayne's peers of the year, there were quite a few lads; they just gelled and they was all of the same in that aspect; of that, you know, when they was together they just wanted a laugh in the classroom regardless; and, you know, it wasn't always Wayne, obviously, but, if Wayne got caught, Wayne was told off and that was where he would kick off as well: "Well you haven't told him," you know, and the usual, you know, of saying, "You blame me all the time," type of thing and it's because you have seen him do it and you haven't seen the others, and it was, it was like that, it was saying, "Well, I'm sorry but, I've seen you doing this and I'm concerned for you, you know, I want you to do well," but that would be it. Wayne got to be a very tall and strong young man and sometimes he could be quite intimidating when, you know, he replied back to you and that. But again I think sometimes it was part of what you had to do for support; obviously just encourage and do what you've got to do.

Interviewer: That's all you can do, though, isn't it?

Jane: Yes it is.

Interviewer: OK, so what happened to Wayne's attendance through school? How did that change from when you first supported him to when you ended up with him?

Jane: Because there was a break in the year that I didn't support so I don't know whether whoever supported him in that year noticed a difference, but definitely by Year 11 I can't recall seeing Wayne very often within the English group. I mean, I can't say about other days. English at that time, obviously, was one hour lessons three times a week, the same for maths and science and I only supported Wayne in English at the time. I know Miss Smith supported him in maths and I think he enjoyed maths better, to be truthful, because I think – again, the basic skills area of it; spellings and certain things he struggled with; but I do, I can't recall seeing Wayne very often in Year 11, to be truthful. But again we are never really told a reason why or whether it's just circumstances that's due to whatever's happened outside or not.

Interviewer: Wayne went through some pretty big changes in Year 11. How do you think that affected him or were you aware of them at the time?

Jane: Not really; wasn't aware of that kind of situation well, any kind of situation, really. I suppose because sometimes you're so involved with other students as well, when you go to support somebody and they don't want it, you do back off a little bit, you can't necessarily sit with them and get to the bottom of everything. Obviously you would ask if they was OK and if they said yeah and just don't want your support, you'd move away, you know, you can't enforce it at the end of the day. They are young men, they are young adults and it's trying to respect their choices as well, really.

Interviewer: Did he ever talk to you about what was happening?

Jane: No.

Interviewer: OK. What sort of support did you give him with his English and maths? What sort of things did he struggle with?

Jane: It would just be basic, 'cause obviously we was doing a lot of coursework and we did the *Romeo and Juliet* piece and we also did, I'm sure it was also a media – it was a media piece on *Romeo and Juliet*. He loved that 'cause obviously they get to watch the Baz Luhrmann film but when they're doing their coursework, even in the media section, they always compare the play but they just look at the film; and again you have got to look at it as the play type of thing and, yeah, they'd understand but when they came to write it down. So, again, it was basic knowledge of making sure spellings were correct, punctuation, capital letters; they used to have a lot of differentiated worksheets anyway, to help them to make sure the structure was OK, you know – and it was ensuring that he was following that so that something good would come out of his end piece of coursework, really.

Interviewer: If you had to describe Wayne overall – as a person at school, at that time – how would you describe him?

Jane: Are we talking about Year 11?

Interviewer: Well...

Jane: Or in general?

Interviewer: Start with how he was at the beginning.

Jane: Well, truthfully, I'd always say, you know – always a very polite young man, you know, except when he had something happen, like any of us would do, truthfully; we all react in different ways; but I've got to say he was always polite, always said thank you and please, you know, or he'd say sorry if you was, like, doing something; he would say sorry – or not necessarily sorry in a bad way, like he's done something bad, but he was trying to explain: "Sorry, miss," sort of thing that he hadn't understood it in that aspect; but no, I would always say that he was very polite to us as members of staff. Obviously if we had a bad day we had Wayne as Wayne, you know, if that was his way of dealing with things, especially if things were happening. It's understandable, I suppose, to a degree, and I think sometimes as members of staff, we need to be informed of things so that everybody can deal with people in a certain way.

Interviewer: Did he have any support at school other than you in his English?

Jane: It would have been mainly the core subjects. I don't know whether he would have had any, you know, mentoring and guidance at the time. I'm sure he would have, but I'm not fully aware of what happened.

Connexions personal adviser's story

Sarah: OK, I first met with Wayne in August 2009. He'd left school in 2008 with very few, low grade GCSE qualifications. Since leaving school, Wayne had participated in a programme called E2E – that is called Entry to Employment – with various training providers but, unfortunately, Wayne had never fully engaged in any of the programmes. The main reason for this was his main concern in providing for his child. He was now a young father with a 1-year-old son, Kevin. Quite understandably, Wayne wanted to get a job or an apprenticeship that paid a reasonable salary, rather than just rely on EMA or benefits. Having spoken to Wayne at great length about this, trying to get him to understand that he wasn't going to be able to get the high-paid jobs because of his low GCSE grades and trying to encourage him to look at training, that was our starting point, really. We discussed improving his qualifications and employability skills; we talked about him engaging on the Entry to Learning programme, which required only part-time attendance – and Wayne was keen on warehouse work and Entry to Learning could engage him on a forklift truck training programme that was something Wayne was quite keen on. He felt that this was a bit of – a more grown-up environment;

more of a grown-up job, if you like, giving him some sort of responsibility. So he did agree to attend an interview to find out more about it. I had also been speaking to Wayne about applying for temporary Christmas vacancies, particularly with Argos, as they would offer the type of work he was actually looking for. Wayne thought this was a good idea and completed an online application in the Connexions centre.

Two weeks later, Wayne came and informed me that he had been invited for a group interview and was very keen on having some interview tips and I arranged for Wayne to call into the Connexions centre to see me to discuss that. Wayne did live at home with Mom, so, obviously, again, it was very important for him to bring in money so him getting this temporary job was – he was hinging on getting this job so he could provide for his child and provide for money at home to sort of take the pressure off from Mom nagging him all the time to get something and do something and also, you know, to try and get a bit of self-worth, really, because Wayne, even though he was quite a personable lad, he was; he hadn't got a lot of confidence and he needed to get that confidence inside of him, really, to prove to himself that he could actually do it; 'cause through school he wasn't the sort of kid that would have engaged in school very much, anyway; didn't really like school, wanted to get out, wanted to do something, you know, like a lot of young people, really, but he sort of lost his way a little bit once he'd actually left school. So a week later in October 2009, Wayne rang to let me know that he had been offered a full-time job on a temporary contract with Argos in Westbury absolutely thrilled to bits, couldn't believe it. Came in with his uniform on, told me that he would get me to the front of the queue if I went in to buy anything – he was just brilliant, he absolutely loved it, couldn't thank me enough, even though I did say to him I hadn't actually done anything; this was all down to him and he needed to recognize the fact that he is capable, really.

In February 2010, Wayne came in to the Connexions centre in Westbury to tell me that, unfortunately, his contract with Argos had actually come to an end. He was gutted, 'cause he really, really thought that, you know, he could be kept on; he was really hopeful of being kept on and obviously he enjoyed the salary, that meant he could spend money on his little boy, on his girlfriend and on his mom – you know, something that he had never really had before. On a positive Wayne did ask if he could be submitted to the Entry to Learning programme again, in order to gain his forklift truck licence. The interest in this had come from his experience of working in Argos and knowing and hoping he could actually go that far and get his licence. And the other big thing for Wayne was the fact that it can cost a lot of money if you are to do it privately because we had talked about the forklift licence before. So using the Entry to Learning programme to his... his end, really, and to get it for nothing if you like, was all the bonus for him, was all the better for him. So what we did was we rang one of the local providers and arranged an appointment for him. We also did some research together about apprenticeships in warehousing 'cause obviously this had sparked a big interest for him now and we discovered a new training provider based in Kings. Wayne was keen to attend, so we rang, we arranged an interview and he attended their centre the following week. He wasn't averse to the fact that the position was in Kingswinford because he's now got his car, he's very mobile – he's just very keen to earn some money and provide for his family, that, again, is the big thing for him. On a positive again, he rang me to let me know that he had been offered a place on their programme to start in the beginning of March. And at that point, as far as I knew, he was actually undertaking his NVQ 2 in Warehouse and Distribution, which would include white goods and everything else, really, and hopefully would gain his forklift licence from that organization.

Interviewer: That's very good.

Sarah: OK.

Interviewer: Can you tell me a little bit about Wayne and how he got on at school and whether he talked to you about his school experience?

Sarah: Right, well, um – I think it is only fair to say that Wayne was very negative about school. He wasn't an academic in any way, shape, or form. Wayne was more of a hands-on kind of kid. He knew that he was capable of something, which is why he has always looked at getting a job and being practical, and the thought, for him, of sitting in a classroom situation doing a college course would have been his worst nightmare, really, to be fair, and wouldn't have moved him on; in fact, I think if he had been encouraged to go to college personally, I think he would have dropped out because I just don't think he would have coped with the situation at all. He's very much a hands-on, very much an, "I want to earn some money, this is what I want to do, I don't want to get qualifications, I just want to get a job."

Interviewer: Yeah.

Sarah: Right.

Interviewer: Do you think that had anything to do with his experience at school? Do you think something...

Sarah: Possibly, possibly. I mean, because he was unengaged I think he used to get in trouble a lot.

Interviewer: Yeah.

Sarah: And I think he used to get a lot of detentions and he used to skive a lot and he used to, you know, be a bad attender and I think that's just had a knock-on effect really. And I think it was a shame that maybe he wasn't given the opportunity to do something as an alternative; you know, maybe through the brokerage service or maybe it wasn't running then, I don't know. But, you know, something like that. But obviously there was always a cost to the school and maybe the school didn't feel it was cost effective, I don't know.

Interviewer: Can you tell me a little bit about his family situation?

Sarah: Yeah, um, he lives at home with Mom and Stepdad and I think he still has contact with Dad, I think, but I wouldn't be a 100 per cent on that. He doesn't really speak about Dad, to be fair. As far as Wayne is concerned his family is baby boy Kevin and his partner Sue. That's his family as far as he is concerned, really, even though he is quite close to Mom. But, you know, he goes to, he gets up early in the morning and goes to Sue's house; they don't live together, they still live very separately with their parents – but he will get up early in the morning, he will go to Sue's, he will take care of Kevin so that Sue can have some time to herself 'cause she has been with him all night, which is quite positive, really.

Interviewer: Yeah.

Sarah: Yeah, he does take his responsibility very seriously, to be fair.

Analysis of citations:
References to low basic skills   12
Low motivation   10 (but 11 references to good motivation)
Unemployment in family   1
Poor behaviour in school   24
LDD (receiving support)   8

Chapter 9

Mia

Mia is of mixed White and African Caribbean heritage. She speaks English as her first language and was raised by her birth mother, who is now living with a new partner. Mia is living at home, and expecting a baby.

Mia's risk-factor score was 11, arising from:

Low basic skills
Low motivation
Unemployment in family
Poor behaviour in school
Poor school attendance
LDD (she was on the SEN Code of Practice)

Interviews were conducted with Mia in a public place and with her mother in their home. Interviews were also conducted with her Connexions personal adviser, the head of the inclusion unit (LSU) at her school and the assistant head, who knew her well. The school has been named Wooding Green for this text.

Timeline for Mia

Date	*Activity*
Sept 2005	Compulsory education
Aug 2009	
Sept 2009	Training provider/foundation learning
Oct 2009	
Nov 2009	
Dec 2009	
Jan 2010	
Feb 2010	NEET
Mar 2010	
Apr 2010	
May 2010	
Jun 2010	
Jul 2010	
Aug 2010	Training provider/foundation learning
Sept 2010	
Oct 2010	
Nov 2010	
Dec 2010	
Jan 2011	
Feb 2011	
Mar 2011	NEET

Apr 2011	
May 2011	
Jun 2011	
Jul 2011	College
Aug 2011	
Sept 2011	
Oct 2011	
Nov 2011	
Dec 2011 – to date	Apprenticeship

Mia's story

Interviewer: Right, Mia. First of all thank you very much for agreeing to do this, it's a real help. Mia, this is about you in school.

Mia: Yeah.

Interviewer: What I want you to do is try and remember the early days of you in school. Just tell me what you remember.

Mia: I used to remember meeting new faces, experiencing very different people and their backgrounds and stuff like that and, like, it helped me to get through school. Certain friends, certain friends bullied, well, I did get bullied at school but you just go through that level, don't ya, at school. But, um, when it's school, shall I say, where do I start. It was good, I did enjoy it; I did like school, it was just, um, I dunno, just like, certain things day bother me, like, lessons, in a way – certain lessons like RE and stuff like that but school was good. I don't know what to say, school was good.

Interviewer: That's fine. Were there any particularly nice teachers or teachers that you didn't get on with?

Mia: Well, my best was my headteacher, Mr Evansure – he was a wicked support, to be honest, through school for me. If he wor[1] there, I don't think I'd be at school to be fair. He was a help and there was Miss Harper, like, an LSU [learning support unit] group class that I was always in 'cause I had problems in lessons, like, got distracted – I'm loud, like, I was loud in

---

[1] wasn't

school so, you know. But, um, and, um, I was always with Miss Harper; she was nice as well – she was a brilliant woman, and her daughter was.

Interviewer: When you said you had difficulties in classes, what kind of difficulties were they?

Mia: Concentrating, really, concentrating to do the work 'cause them times as a kid I wor interested, I wor bothered, just woke up in a foul mood and I day want to do it, I day want to go to school; but certain days I did enjoy myself – I did actually like certain classes like drama. Stuff like that I did enjoy myself.

Interviewer: Were there any classes that you really didn't get on with?

Mia: I'd say maths. Maths is quite hard for me 'cause I'm a bit down on my maths but I do try, that's all I can do; but maths is the worst for me, yeah.

Interviewer: As you went through the school, did things get better? Did things get worse? You mentioned the head was kind to you.

Mia: Yeah.

Interviewer: As you got older through the school what happened?

Mia: What do you mean?

Interviewer: Was it easier as you got older in school? Or was that harder?

Mia: It wasn't any different, to be honest, it was, like, yesterday to me – I can just remember it like it was yesterday. It was no different, apart from the new buildings and teachers coming in to the school. That was different and people day[2] – like, some kids don't, like, react well with teachers, do they? 'Cause certain teachers day, dunno, treat you in that manner that you wanna be treated, really. But you just have to go along with it 'cause it's school. And at the end of the day you just go home and go back to school. It was OK, though – I did enjoy myself.

Interviewer: What happened when you left school? What happened at the end of Year 11?

Mia: I left school and I was thinking, well, I – the first few months after school I day[3] do nothing. I was like, I ay[4] bothered, I ay doing nothing, that's how I felt. But, like, I woke up and I went to go to Connexions one day and I was asking for a bit of help, like where can I go and what can I start? And they put me on a few training courses, so I tried 'em out, done some qualifications off them, like, and then, like, um, I had a contact from this centre I was at with Connexions about Jane Oak and stuff like that. They

---

[2] didn't
[3] didn't
[4] I'm not

moved me on to something else but I found this from Connexions as well. So, I like to try new things out and see what it brings me, really. It's different.

Interviewer: So what kind of things are you doing here now?

Mia: Well, what I was doing first was web design and designing stuff but now I want to change and do masks and painting and stuff like that. Get my hands dirty [laughs]. I like to be active I like to do things instead of, like, writing things.

Interviewer: That sounds great fun. And you're going to be a mom shortly?

Mia: Yeah, be a mom soon, yeah. Nerve-wracking, scared, but that's life.

Interviewer: Thank you very much.

Mia's mother's story

Interviewer: Right, fine. We are here to talk about your daughter Mia. Tell us what you remember – particularly regarding school – right from the beginning.

Mother: Mia's first school was White Croft and at the time the nursery school was under threat of closure and there was a community centre that was adjacent to it where I took Mia for the moms' and toddlers' club. Mia was ill at the time; she had to spend a lot of time in and out of hospital as she had a growth on her face. Um, her mouth was open, as they call a daytime snorer. She also started having fits at the age of 4 after she had an operation to remove the growth. Then, in between that, the school – the nursery school – had been closed by the council. I'd moved back down to Wednesdale and she went to Hale Field nursery school for a short time, where they said they couldn't cope with her because she was a deaf child and as well at that time she kept dropping and having a fit. There was then a school called Hill Garden in Wednesdale that had smaller numbers in the class. I was also involved with the education of deaf children and for normal educated children where we was having meetings. This school seemed like with only a few kids in the class; they could accommodate her. I used to attend school with her most days and as she got older she developed asthma but she was on steroids and put weight on.

We encouraged her to do sport – she got involved with the football ground and dancing with a teacher at the school. She went, um, went and did the pitch in front of 32,000 spectators and scored a goal with her dad. That was a charity match for *Fight against Racism*. I said the education was under the threat of closure of schools, the education was changing for the children and I was already having a problem with Mia with her hearing and so, like, I fought really hard to keep her in mainstream school. She's done really well.

Happy child most of the time; kept up with everything, normally in fact, she was in front with her reading and writing and they said they were really pleased with her at the school.

Then she went to Wooding Green and she got on in Wooding Green purely on her merit; like, she passed her exams, like, to go in and so there was no problem of, like, she didn't have to go into the bottom set or anything like that. She went in, like, middle to top but, um, as her behaviour with her complications and stuff they didn't really understand her, so she had a lot of, um, complications within the classroom because she couldn't, like, socialize really because of, like, spending a lot of time in hospital and, um, not really socializing with other kids. She believed whatever they told her was the gospel truth; she couldn't cope with the fact that they was telling her lies or that children can be cruel and, like, she was having a lot of name-calling and obviously she couldn't hear a lot so I suppose that helped her in a way. But, um, I was down the school quite a bit. She had a lot of support off, um, the teachers down there and, um, they kept me informed daily of all of her progress of whatever she was doing and that. And she was fine and the teachers at the school, you know, gave support to us, like, when she was in hospital and stuff so, you know, she had her work to carry on with and she done it no matter how ill she was she would always do her homework and get everything up to date.

And she tried really hard, she got involved, since she had the operation to remove the growth from her face and they said it would come back, but Mia tried a lot of breathing techniques and things and they said it would affect her eyes but the flatness of her nose sort of evened itself out and her eyes. She stopped wearing glasses and she was wearing them and then, um, she got involved in sports at school and doing with, uh, the fire station in Wednesdale. And her favourite fireman was Mr Lucie at the fire station; he is head of the fire station. I think he is a station manager now or something. He took all the girls from there who were normally interested in the fire station and stuff and Mia was one of the girls that was interested in fire station stuff and boy sort of stuff. So, like I say, she then got more involved in the football but unfortunately, because of her breathing and everything else, she couldn't really carry on with it. But she done it intermittently; usually she does, anyway like, when she can.

Interviewer: Can I just ask how many times you moved house?

Mother: Um, twice.

Interviewer: Right. And did you move house at all when she was at secondary school?

Mother: No.

Interviewer: You've been here all the time.

Mother: Constantly, yep.

Interviewer: OK. Had she had any idea of what she wanted to do? A job or training?

Mother: She wanted to do travel and tourism from an early age. She wanted to go off and see the world. She wanted to get out there because she's led quite a sheltered life; that everything is organized for her. That's why she's had problems since being a teenager with, um, like she's got a white brother. I mean, recently her and her brother got arrested because she's pregnant and she's going to the garage at ten o'clock at night and they walked through a gulley, her and her brother, and he's white and she's half-caste, quite dark. They was going to the garage at ten o'clock, half ten, and, uh, come back and they both got arrested because they didn't believe they were brother and sister and there was something going on in the area and they just – they kept 'um on a curfew for a couple of months. These are the sorts of things that have happened to Mia all her life. She's in the wrong place at the wrong time; situations happen that she's got no idea about but she's there in some way and there's been a lot of cases like that.

She did have, uh, I'd say, not a criminal record, it's just carried on; you know, I've been involved with the probation service from, like, obviously not really criminal activities or anything that she's done. It's mainly 'cause of her attitude and the way she is and it's like I've followed that through with her and tried to keep the authorities informed of what's happening because it ain't even been, it's been the people she's associated with from the special schools, from the same situation as what she was, but have gone somewhere else and have gone through deaf school, or you know. I mean, she's got a friend that we call Bart and his real name is Brian but we've – Mia's known him since about 5 years old; they was up town and shopping quite recently and they went shopping for make-up, she'd been in Connexions and I was actually on the phone to the man in Connexions when they left. The police surrounded them because they didn't believe Mia was a girl, and they'd stopped them for shoplifting down the town with some make-up, lipstick, one lipstick. The man in Connexions on the phone to me was saying, "I can't believe it, she's just spoken to me and walked outside the door and the police have surrounded her." Then they got her and twisted her up across a verge and it's camera-ed,[5] in't it, so we insisted on seeing the cameras. They kept her in the police cells for about three or four hours and I was going mad 'cause she has her inhalers and everything else and, um, we're going to a thing. I

---

[5] recorded

could tek it further with the police because of the situation here we are again, back to square one because Mia is associated with people that are disabled and community police and the authorities don't understand that these kids, youngsters, teenagers, are out there on the streets and yeah, OK, there's no excuse and you hold your hands up if a child or an adult is stealing from shops or whatever – it's an offence or whatever – but it's not an offence to walk around shouting, in Mia's case 'cause she does, 'cause she's deaf, not 'cause she's shouting being aggressive; she's shouting because she can't hear her own voice and obviously she's loud. Mia's been in a lot of trouble because of her loudness and I found that at school with her, but she's been fine; like I say, every day is a fight with her and she is determined on what she wants to do and she will succeed. I got every faith in her.

Interviewer: A couple more questions. Is there anyone in the family that is unemployed? Anyone that hasn't got a job?

Mother: My son, but he's in college still.

Interviewer: So do you have a job?

Mother: I'm sick at the moment. I've had an accident.

Interviewer: OK, right.

Mother: But I will be going back to work.

Interviewer: Fine, OK. What was her attendance like at school?

Mother: As good as it could be.

Interviewer: Right.

Mother: Yeah, but if there was anything, like, she couldn't. The school knew and they'd phone me sometimes to come and fetch her 'cause they; that teacher down the school just knew, could tell by Mia's face, 'cause her face changed, you know, if she was going to fit; or as she's got older she can feel it coming on herself. But she always kept up with all her school work and that. Always a positive reaction off everybody: friends with everybody and everything. Everybody knows Mia. I think partly because she is loud and because of the way she is, that's it. She's had quite a few tragedies; a few school friends have killed themselves. A friend that she met through an out-of-school activity within the borough of Wednesdale, sort of a half-caste, 'cause, you see, I've got a white son and like everything's English around her, sort of thing, and I wanted her to have a bit of culture and because she was asking, like it's part of who she is, you know, and everything else.

Well you know I wanted her to find out and meet friends, you know, other girls that are probably having situations like you are, you know, have a chat. That got her involved in, like, a work group thing. There was some young girls there of her own age and different nationalities and everything, so it was just a melting pot of having fun and I think that's what kids growing up that have got problems need all the time. You know, and get her to think positive 'cause it's hard for her sometimes to just get up and I used to go mental and say, you know, "Do something" and I'd be, like, really agitated and mad with her and everything until the doctors told me but I still didn't stop, I have to admit, because they told me that, like, "Oh, she's got chronic this and chronic that.' I should have been a bit more understanding, but unless, you know; and at the same time I think you have to deal every day with a child growing up and being sick. 'Cause my life has never been my own since the day she's been born. I've never had a good night's sleep with her and always; every day is a drama in some way. You know, I've got to be on call for her; it's like, it's no good thinking, "Well, oh, I'll do this this morning," or whatever and making arrangements. Yeah I can do things, but when I start to do something, there's always a phone call or she gets herself worked up in such a state. She can't always tell if she's going to flip and I always think if she has a little moan and a dig at me it's not gonna go out there.

And it's worked because, um – talking of psychology, I went and seen a few people about psychology and it just bamboozled me, like, whatever they was telling me. I was trying it on my daughter and it wasn't working so, I mean, I just sort of tried this, go with the flow, you know, and try something else. I think it's just part of the development of a child growing up as well. I think, me and myself – I think as a parent you can be too protective of your children and then when things do sort of happen and that it's to a different degree because you have protected your child because they are sick, but, you know, I mean – like I say every day is just a trial with her and she tried really hard at everything she does: she puts 150 per cent she does – she puts her heart and soul in everything she does because she's that sort of child. She's that sort of young adult now and I've got every confidence in her in everything she tries. I mean, I've been so surprised about her singing because of her having the operation on her face and her breathing and her voice itself. She's been amazing because to look at her and the way she speaks, to hear her voice singing, it's like a totally different person and I'm really proud of her and I'll carry on supporting her.

Mia's school's story – Jane, LSU and Adam, DHT

Interviewer: OK, Jane, tell me about Mia, and if we can start from your earliest memories, how was she when she came to school and when she first came to your attention?

Jane: She came to my attention in Year 8. Her behaviour was a bit erratic. She was referred to the LSU by her head of year for a meeting with Mr King and myself. Mia was very complex; she was put into LSU because she had a very complex outlook on life and couldn't focus very well with being told what to do within a classroom setting; that was her main referral problem. Um, very loud, very aggressive, very confrontational towards rules, regulations and conforming to any adult forms of rules. Home life was also an issue at that time as well, because Mom and Dad were together but were going to split and Mia was finding that a little difficult. But the relationship Mom and Dad were in; you couldn't really put your finger on their relationship, as they were saying they were apart but then they'd be doing things. Mia would say they were doing things as a family, going out. Mia was getting mixed messages, very confusing for her as at that age, 12–13 years old; she found that difficult, which bought into school issues with adults 'cause of the mixed messages adults were giving. Mia was very confrontational with peers – good at having a good fight, language very blue and nothing that she couldn't put her tongue to; not really scared of anyone in any situation; would always come out fighting would be her reaction. She went into sort of red mist areas where she was sort of backing herself into a corner so she had to fight to be able to try and get herself out of the situations.

Interviewer: What do you mean by red mist areas?

Jane: Where she just focused into a tunnel of a red-coloured mist. It's what I usually say when our kids have gone into a rage and that's where she used to put herself – back herself into a corner so that she couldn't find a way out unless it was verbally, rude fighting, to be able to – to not lose face with anyone around her that may have been viewing her. Very strong willed young lady so it was difficult, at times, to reason with her until she'd come out of this red mist and you allowed her time. And she'd come back and sit down then and speak with you – and she'd usually say, "I'm sorry, I shouldn't have said those words," and understand that she had gone past the level of normality for a young lady to behave, shall we say. And she would apologize – and then you would have her as a typical average young lady for a little while; once she'd blown she seemed to be average for a few, say, for a day or two. She'd be quite OK. But Mia is very erratic and doesn't look at things very easily, um, out of a box; she's always in the box and always sees everything as a big issue and that it's people picking on her and telling her what to do and she didn't like it at all. As I've said before it was a big issue with Mia that she was told what to do. Mom would let her have a lot of her own way to save the confrontation at home. Mom and me built up a working relationship that Mom would phone me and tell me if there had been a problem at home and likewise I would ring Mom and inform her if we had any issues at school with Mia.

As the years progressed, Mia of course was developing and being more sociable with boys and groups of people – I was aware that Mia was mixing with a very unsociable group outside of school that did drugs and displayed anti-social behaviour. Mia was quite happy to live in that world 'cause she did like a good argument, I would say; she seemed to relish it, that she was showing how tough she was and that nobody was gonna make her feel and she would go after them, you know, deliberately to make them intimidated by her. So she liked the anti-social behaviour group that she was in and she sort of liked that strength of where they lived and how she could perform. She was quite happy to be there. Family life got less difficult because Dad was living somewhere else by this time and she saw Dad. There were still mixed messages, though, because Mom and Dad still did things together sometimes, so Mia didn't really get that Mom and Dad were totally split, that they were sort of, at times together; so Mia's life would be very confusing for her still.

She grew into this really confrontational, verbally aggressive person. She was small in height, quite a plump young lady, but not fat, um, very pretty, you know, so she fits socially. But she wasn't an overly girly girl up until she got to about 15 and then started wearing some make-up; before then she was more like, um, one of the boys type thing and would act similar to a boy actually, with her general behaviour. But from 15, make-up started to go on, she bothered with her hair, jewellery was more available to her and so you could see she was growing up. She was developing sexually as well I would say within the group she socialized with in the evenings, which to me made Mia very vulnerable because even though she portrayed herself to be this maturer young lady, she was not really a mature young lady and was very immature in how she dealt with situations and dealing with any problems that came her way. She always reverted to a younger stage of how to deal with it that was, again, verbally aggressive, rude, and confrontational. This was Mia's main aim all the time and it didn't improve from her leaving.

Interviewer: What did she go on to? What were her ambitions?

Jane: Well, Mia didn't really know what she wanted to do; she had no idea of forward thinking because Dad didn't work, Mom didn't work, they were both at home and the people she socialized with were unemployed people. The older boys didn't do anything, college or anything; they just sort of "dossed around", to use their words, and did not really do anything that, um, improved life really. Drugs were more apparent in their world 'cause some of the young guys she was mixing with were selling things, so in her world you didn't have to work to earn some cash.

Interviewer: What was her attendance like?

Jane: Quite good, really, quite good. And some days you'd wish that she didn't turn up, if you know what I mean – especially if you'd had a bad day with her before, with her being really confrontational with staff. You kind of hoped to maybe have a time-out and a bit of a breather but Mia would come to school; she would only be away mainly for exclusions, yes.

Interviewer: Were there any difficulties with reading and writing?

Jane: Yes, more with her phonics, her written skills were not so bad – she had quite nice handwriting because Mia did like things to look right, even though she couldn't spell a word; she'd always ask you to spell the word 'cause she knew she couldn't spell it. But her reading was poor.

Interviewer: Right.

Jane: Especially with more difficult texts.

Interviewer: And as far as you are aware, was she always living in the same house?

Jane: Yes.

Interviewer: That's fine.

Jane: Yeah.

Interviewer: OK. Is there anything else you would like to add?

Jane: Only that I know from leaving school she began attending Jane Oak. I think that she went to that in Woodbury but heard that she still wasn't engaging very well with having to do things, of course, and then ending up in the situation she's in now. She hasn't changed, she still spends most of her time in a pub and is smoking and drinking, so not even now she's pregnant is she taking on board any different lifestyle changes to protect the baby.

Interviewer: OK. Jane, thank you very much indeed.

Adam: I can't add anything to that, can I?

Jane: Only that you've had words with her about her general behaviour.

Adam: All those were inside there.

Jane: I think I could pick her up right this minute – and I've had a break from her – but I'd still know how she was thinking and how to put or implement some differentiation with her because she would not have changed her mindset of how things work.

Adam: I can't think of anything. The only thing was that it was almost a no-go with some stuff; so challenging – staff felt quite intimidated if she was in their presence because she wouldn't accept boundaries, and she was verbally, not physically, threatening, but that just her whole demeanour was threatening to staff. So that it did get to a stage where some staff were quite scared of her, weren't they?

Jane: Yeah, and we reduced her timetable so she was mainly in the LSU and not out so much.

Adam: You've summarized well what was going on in her life and some.

Jane: I've been a little polite [laughs].

Adam: Her language was absolutely...

Jane: And also what she got up to...

Adam: And she'd go from nought to ten straight away, wouldn't she?

Jane: Yeah, oh yeah.

Adam: She would just blow up and then come back.

Jane: It wasn't like a progression of temper. She would just speed into that temper.

Connexion's worker's story

Interviewer: Thanks. We are here to talk about Mia and let's start from the beginning. What do you remember? What kind of involvement has Connexions had with her?

Connexions: Most of my involvement started from school, where there were some issues in school, and with our support we identified a brokerage scheme where she could spend a couple of days with a training provider. This was called Jane Oak; it was because she wanted to do hairdressing and beauty. So she was still engaged in education at the time. She quite enjoyed doing that and I think that was probably where the career carried on from that. She still likes to do hair and beauty, even now. From the brokerage and leaving school she attended a training provider in order to get her maths and English and IT grades up, as she didn't really have grades when leaving school. Our support was really more for her educational needs. There were also personal issues, which I don't think I should discuss here, because some of that was confidential and I don't have her permission to do that. However, it was mainly to do with her image and identity – how she is seen by other people – and also there was no support or support mechanism, i.e. a counselling agency that she could access so that she could deal with those issues. So what we did – as it was not just myself, but also other colleagues from the Connexions agency – was helped to support her through the transition from school where she actually ended up at a training provider in Woodbury. This was not far from where she lives and that was due to the fact that we felt it was best for her to be really close to home because of her identity issues. She had a short fuse so sometimes she would lash out and she knew that, she knew about that. We put something in place for her to access in order for her to address those behavioural issues. Every training provider that she went to, we informed them of that and that was with Mia's consent.

From leaving that one provider in W with all her grades intact – i.e. her grades in literacy, numeracy, and ICT – she then moved on to another provider where she is doing digital imagery. The reason that she is doing that course at the moment is that she needed some money coming in and she had this fear of college, but she has now identified in herself that she really wants to go for the college route and do leisure and tourism because she feels as though all the internalized issues that she felt about herself led to the behaviour being quite bad. However, she said, "I can do it, I will do it," and that is where she is at at the moment.

She is six-and-a-half months pregnant and she felt that it might hold her back. After her exploration she realized (because I shared some of my views with her) that I got back into education after having my fourth child, as a mature student and so she sort of realized that she could still do it. I came out of university with a degree and I explained that to her. She thought, "right" and that's probably why she is sticking her head forward and knows that she can achieve that.

Interviewer: Good stuff. Now we are just going to go through a few things. Her accommodation is stable, she hasn't moved house a lot. What about her motivation? Did she have a clear idea of what she wanted to do?

Connexions: She had an idea of what she wanted to do from school. That was part of the brokerage programme that I mentioned – the agency which did hair and beauty; because she used to wear a lot of make-up; because she used to feel that covering her identity would make her into somebody different. So she preferred, she continued to do that. That's why she chose the hair and beauty arena, because it was all about make-up and covering that image. The motivation was very, very low due to the fact that she said she had some issues not just with young people – her peers – but also with teachers and other agencies that she was in contact with, who she felt well, she felt were looking at her in a hopeless way. But that was part of her paranoia because of what she felt about herself, so she was low-motivated. She had a boyfriend that, I think, made her motivation even lower. He died, just recently, of cancer and they knew about this prior to that. There were some issues that I can't go into around that, but her motivation got lower because he was the person who was there for her, who loved her, that believed in her.

With him leaving her motivation got even lower; but now she is with a new partner who is also supporting her. She is pregnant now, and her motivation has got higher and I do believe that part of it came from helping her get that motivation up initially. This came from Mia herself and my experience of being a single mother, also sharing my own experience of coming from a family of 15 where the mom had four children. I'm the third child from a different father. My mom remarried and I was brought up in a stepfamily, so we shared some similar issues. I was able to say that

I understand where you are coming from because I've been there myself. So she was quite pleased that she wasn't the only person on the planet that was feeling that way; at that age I was feeling that way. I felt that somehow I had to give back to the family. I didn't learn that, until later in life, that I didn't have to give back because I was part of the family. The motivation came from that really.

Interviewer: Lovely. Is there anything you would like to add?

Connexions: No, but I feel that Mia has grown so much. It's a shame that she wasn't followed from an earlier age to see that growth. But I think that research like this should go back further, lower, and see the growth and see the obstacles that are around, rather than say, "They are lazy, just want to get pregnant," type of thing.

Analysis of citations:

Accommodation changes	1
References to low basic skills	3
Low motivation	7
Unemployment in family	2
Poor behaviour in school	21
LDD (receiving support)	1
Known to youth offending team	3
Poor school attendance	3

Chapter 10

Kevin

Kevin is black, speaks English as his first language and was raised by his birth mother. Kevin and his mother live together and have just moved into a house. Previously, they were sharing a house with other members of their extended family.

Kevin's risk-factor score was 15, arising from:

Changes in accommodation
Known to the youth offending team
Low motivation
Unemployment in family
Poor basic skills
Poor behaviour in school
LDD (he was on the SEN code of practice)
Poor school attendance

Interviews were conducted with Kevin and his mother in their home. Interviews were also conducted with his Connexions personal adviser, an assistant head who knew Kevin, a mentor who worked in the Learning Support Unit, and a sports mentor. The school has been named James Hill Academy for this text.

Timeline for Kevin

Date	Activity
Sept 2009	Compulsory education
Sept 2010	Compulsory education
Aug 2011	NEET
Sept 2011	NEET
Oct 2011	Training provider/foundation learning
Nov 2011	Training provider/foundation learning
Dec 2011	Training provider/foundation learning
Jan 2012	Training provider/foundation learning
Feb 2012	Training provider/foundation learning
Mar 2012	Training provider/foundation learning
Apr 2012	Apprenticeship
May 2012	Apprenticeship
Jun 2012	Apprenticeship
Jul 2012 – to date	Apprenticeship

Kevin's story

Interviewer: Kevin, this is about you in school and what I want to do is for you to go back. You were at Taper's Green?

Kevin: Yeah – Taper's Green.

Interviewer: Just tell me what you remember about Taper's Green and then we will go on to James Hill Academy.

Kevin: Taper's Green – I used to be in a lot of trouble. I was always in the headteacher's office, always fighting, arguments with the teacher; I didn't like sharing, didn't like, I don't know; like, socializing with other people – boys were, like, stuck up, no manners, but, like, I don't know, I just used to fight. I would fight every day. That's about it. I was always in trouble, constantly, twenty four seven, always late, stuff like that.

Interviewer: And what happened when you went to James Hill Academy?

Kevin: I went to James Hill Academy, like, and my mom spoke to me – she spoke to me and said, "You got to fix up – like, you're growing up now." So at high school, I tried coming in more on time and not get, like, a bad record for lates and stuff like that. So then I started coming in, like, sometimes and sometimes late, but I tried, I contributed, but then – yet again I'd a couple of fights, always in isolation. That's where the naughty kids go, basically being in trouble and arguments with teachers, disagreements, running around making noises in the corridor, like, the silly, stupid stuff, hanging round with the wrong people. I had to ditch some of the friends. Always in trouble again, but since I like got into Year 11, I started fixing up, like. Started thinking and changing my life, kind of got into my running and stuff in Year 11 and that was the sport I enjoyed and, like, something to do, something to keep me out of trouble. And, like, I enjoyed that a lot and I wouldn't want to mess it up and stuff – so kind of stopped going out and stuff and messing about and stuff like that. I basically, like, turned around.

Interviewer: Who were the staff that helped you? Were there any?

Kevin: Yeah, there was always Diane – Diane, yeah. Diane was always helping me out. Diane Bates was helping me out and Ms Tearway always helped me. Mr Ground: always, like, headteacher, but he always, like – he's a nice man. He'll say things like, "You're on your last chance," and then I got proper scared and started behaving. You can also have a laugh and a joke. He'd say, "Just get your head down and whilst you are messing around, these people are here to help. You need to be responsible and try and sort it out." Then I was going into Year 11 from 10 and then I started, like, changing. Diane Bates and Ms Tearway and, oh, what's her name?

Interviewer: Mrs Canning?

Kevin: Yes, she helped as well. And the one that works with Diane.

Interviewer: The shorter lady?

Kevin: Yes. What's her name? Anyway there were a load of people.

Interviewer: You left school at the end of Year 11. What happened then?

Kevin: Left school. I thought, some of my friends were just going to sit back and rest a year and just chill and stuff like that, and then I was thinking about just doing the same thing, but, I don't know. For a couple of months, two, three months I went out and stuff. I was being round people that smoked and it was affecting my running and stuff like that. I thought, "Come on, this is killing me, it's not good for me," and stuff, so I thought I would do something. I went to, like, go for jobs and got declined and stuff like that and they said, "No thanks, don't want you." I went to loads of places, made loads of CVs, trying to improve. I asked other friends who said, "Do your CV and improve it online."

I got my CV done and got a bit lost and then I couldn't find anywhere to go and then one day a friend told me about Connexions, which is a company that helps young kids to find places to do stuff like that, so I went down and they spoke to me and said what am I into and I told them about my sport and that and they asked about other things in case that didn't work out – something to fall back on, but I don't know other stuff that I like, 'cause I've got problems with my reading and writing so they said, "Yeah, go to BTC and college," and so I went there and they spoke to me and showed me around the place and I thought, "Ah, I'm not like the only person that feels they haven't got a place." They showed me around, made me feel, like, and no worries – and I was like, yeah. And then I started going there and started looking for, like, a part-time job at the same time because I wasn't earning any money and I didn't want to go out and, like, commit crime to get money, you know what I mean. So, yeah, don't go and get bad. Some of the people in the school thought, "Yeah, Kevin's going to be in prison, yeah," stuff like that. So basically I just want to prove them wrong – I'm going to be someone up there in the world. So I got a job in the Gallery which is really good, nice. So I come here. I do four days here and I've just left my college. I'm going to Sandhurst College now to do my NVC maths to get them grade Cs. Going there and I'll see what happens after that. And my running – looking to be the next Daley Thompson, really. That's my goal before anything else in life. That's where I'm heading.

Kevin's mother's story

Interviewer: This is about your son Kevin and what we want to do is to ask you some questions about your son in school. I want to go back to his primary school days. Do you remember which primary school he went to?

Mother: Taper's Green.

Interviewer: And how did he get on there?

Mother: Quite well – a bit, er, you know, but teacher and student get on quite well.

Interviewer: Did he have any special teachers that he liked?

Mother: Yes, Miss Bright.

Interviewer: Did he get on all right with his reading and writing and things like that?

Mother: No, he did actually have support from the school with that – special teacher to help him with his reading and I think Miss Bright was one of these people. Miss Bright actually called Kevin "her baby". Up until today she still enquires about Kevin and when Kevin pops in and sees her, she says, "How's my baby doin?"

Interviewer: [Laughs] That's lovely, isn't it?

Mother: Yes, it is.

Interviewer: I know Miss Bright, yes.

Mother: Lovely lady.

Interviewer: So which secondary school did he go to?

Mother: Erm, he went to James Hill Academy.

Interviewer: Yes. And how did he get on there?

Mother: Erm, he had a bit of trouble there as well with his reading and writing and they try to give him the support again there to move on but I've seen there he become a bit far away and his reading and writing got a bit better – more than I expected [laughs].

Interviewer: Right. So he came on better than you thought?

Mother: Yes.

Interviewer: That's good – that's nice to hear. What about his behaviour? Did he get in any trouble there? Was he OK?

Mother: He used to get in silly things, really [laughs], messing about, sometimes I'd have to phone, you know, because of fighting in school; playing had turned into something else – but, you know, boys will be boys.

Interviewer: Indeed. Was he sent home? Was he excluded at all?

Mother: Yes. He was excluded once for three days I think but he went back eleven till five in the afternoon.

Interviewer: Oh, right. So he went for the late session/alternative?

Mother: Yes.

Interviewer: Did he manage to stay the course right the way through?

Mother: Yes, he did.

Interviewer: And did he get any exams?

Mother: Yes he got exams.

Interviewer: What sort of exam results did he get?

Mother: I don't quite remember what was his levels when he finish.

Interviewer: That's OK. And what about when he left school?

Mother: When he left school... before he finished school he was interested in athletics; he always go to training and things like that. I think he did get some support from school towards his training. He go to Bounty Academy.

Interviewer: Yes.

Mother: From there, then, when he finish school he decided that he wanted to do something else and he start with this apprenticeship thing. From there he carries on and he's doing his apprenticeship and then he move on to – what do you call that place in town? It's a pink or purple building; I think its pink, you know that big… is it The Gallery?

Interviewer: Oh, I know.

Mother: Yes. He's working at there now.

Interviewer: And what was the apprenticeship for? Can you remember?

Mother: To further his education, yeah.

Interviewer: And that was over in town?

Mother: No, it's West Ville.

Interviewer: So was there any time between the apprenticeship and school where he wasn't doing anything?

Mother: No. He tried to keep himself quite busy; training, apprenticeship and then starting to earn a bit of money for himself.

Interviewer: OK. What I'm trying to work out is that sometimes young people have times when they might be in training but not actually in a job or he might be in training as an apprentice. Did Kevin have that?

Mother: He – I think no, he was just… After he finished school he struggled a bit to find out what he wanted to do because he was signed up to go back to James Hill and then he was thinking – would it be best for me to go back there? Yeah, then he saw the apprenticeship thing somewhere and he said, "I might sign up for the apprenticeship." Because he said in James Hill the things that he want to do – it don't make no sense to stay back and repeat a year. So he just moved on and try to get the places, he don't always get through, he gets rejected – but he continues trying.

Interviewer: Yes, that's what I'd heard; that there was a time when he wasn't sure what he wanted to do.

Mother: Yes.

Interviewer: Now I have some very odd questions to ask you. We're sitting here in your new house and when I came to see you last you were with your mom.

Mother: [Laughs.]

Interviewer: Have you had many changes of house over the past few years?

Mother: Erm, I have been in this country since 2001 and since then I've moved one, two, three, times.

Interviewer: Has Kevin been with you each time you've moved?

Mother: Yes.

Interviewer: So when was the last time before this that you moved?

Mother: About one year and three months.

Interviewer: So that's while he was still at school?

Mother: Yes.

Interviewer: And before that. Can you remember?

Mother: Erm, I spend five years at one house.

Interviewer: So that was quite stable?

Mother: Yes [laughs].

Interviewer: Did Kevin have any attendance problems? Did he always go to school?

Mother: Yes, sometimes he got attendance problems – they would have to phone me from school and say, "Where is Kevin?" [laughs]. We did have a bit of a problem at home as well about him going and family problems brings him down. I'm quite surprised to know that the things that happened have made him determined to move on. Because I always said to them determination is the key because you get kicked down so many times and once you learn how to brush off and go, you will survive [laughs].

Interviewer: Yes, very true. Were there times when he didn't know what he wanted to do?

Mother: Erm – it started before he left James Hill; he was struggling and, you know, he don't know what to do; sending applications to different places, get rejected and things like that.

Interviewer: Is any member of his family or your family unemployed? At the moment, or has been over the last year?

Mother: I am unemployed at the moment.

Interviewer: Have you been looking for work?

Mother: Not yet. I'm trying to settle into this place because moving from the house before then – it was really a struggle. Things happen while we have to move and from there I wasn't working and being there, three bedroom, all of us being there is a struggle. In moving here I am going on to set up my own business; go on to have my own business.

Interviewer: So what are you going to do?

Mother: I can cook very well.

Interviewer: Good!

Mother: I want to have a little café or something like that.

Sports mentor's story

Interviewer: So we're talking about Kevin here. Tell me, how long have you known Kevin?

Sports Mentor: I've known Kevin since he started here in Year 7, so I've known him six years. Erm, and Kevin's always been a loveable rogue; obviously I work within sports so I work with those who often don't get on with the academic subjects but give you a bit more in sports and Kevin falls into that category.

Interviewer: Did he get in trouble? You talk about "loveable rogue".

Sports Mentor: Well, that's probably a statement of, er, yeah… Kevin and his school life in terms of the rules – what to do and where to be – was not really for him. However, he had the freedom of, "I'm quite good at sports; this is where I'm going to excel," and was probably the best memory of Kevin being here.

Interviewer: OK. So what specifically did you do with Kevin?

Sports Mentor: Specifically with Kevin; Kevin had great talent for running, erm, and probably November 2010 I signposted him into an athletics club through a contact of mine. I took him myself along with a couple of his friends who probably weren't as talented as him but just to get him there. From there his talent kind of blossomed. Now the downside of most clubs and environments was there's a cost involved and a commitment to it. So what I did with Kevin was I paid for his role for three months and then basically after the three months it was down to him.

Interviewer: And did he relate particularly well to other people in the sports department?

Sports Mentor: In general, yeah. His relationship was good down there because he was talented and he had time for that subject and that was his interest.

Interviewer: OK. I'm going to go through some risk factors and I want your comment on how you think Kevin would have fared with this. In terms of his motivation and in terms of his ambition when he left school, how would you have described that?

Sports Mentor: His ambition to be the best in athletics would have been excellent. His ambition, maybe, to get on with getting a job and other things would not have been as strong as his athletics ambition.

Interviewer: And would the members of staff at the school have suggested that his behaviour at school was problematic?

Sports Mentor: Yes. Often with kids of that nature over the years staff will say "Ron or Mr Stanton can you have a word with …? And see what you can do?"

Interviewer: What would you say about Kevin's basic skills?

Sports Mentor: I'd probably say Kevin is cleverer than he thinks. However, he lacks confidence in something he may not have full subject knowledge of. He can communicate well but maybe putting that down on a piece of paper or in an exam – that would be where he would struggle.

Interviewer: What was his attendance like?

Sports Mentor: Kevin's attendance [laughs] – you would probably see him at half ten most days, that's Kevin.

Interviewer: What relationship did you have with his family?

Sports Mentor: I knew his brother, who was called Carl, his younger brother who's here; met Mom once or twice. Really, that would be my overview of Kevin – what I know of him and his wider family.

Interviewer: And what do you know of Kevin now?

Sports Mentor: Kevin now? Well Kevin, as I said on the phone – he come to the Olympics with me on 3 August 2012. We won a competition with Coca-Cola by using Kevin as an example of the same things that this interview is about: using someone's talents and being there at the right moment with the right support as a case of good practice. From that we got two tickets from Coca-Cola for the athletics trackside, which I thought, "Who would benefit most from going? – Kevin". Because it was something else to inspire him on for his ambition and love of athletics really.

Interviewer: Is there anything else you would like to add?

Sports Mentor: No, not really, just that Kevin now; his ambition and his goal in life was to be the fastest person in the world and, really, he's the thirty-second best 400m runner in the country for the under-20s and he's 16 now, so he's got four years, so he's on track to do that.

Inclusion manager's story

Interviewer: Just remind us of your role in the school.

Inclusion Manager: I am the Centre of Inclusion manager at James Hill Academy.

Interviewer: And we're here to talk about Kevin and I want you to go back as far as you can. To Year 7, if you can go back that far.

Inclusion Manager: Yes.

Interviewer: What are your memories of the young Kevin?

Inclusion Manager: Erm, Kevin came to us on repeated occasions, normally for petty misdemeanours; he was always a bit of a Jack the Lad and was always up to some mischief somewhere along the line. And we run an isolation provision at James Hill, so more often than not he was visiting isolation to do some stints up there. Because of that he was also placed on some of our behaviour programmes in the Centre of Inclusion to try and sort of look at the areas of behaviour that we needed to improve. So he did spend quite a lot of his time in Key Stage 3 in and out of the Centre of Inclusion with small group work, behaviour programmes and other sort of provisions that we run up there.

Interviewer: How was he socially within the school?

Inclusion Manager: Kevin was always a really popular young man; he's one of these young men that I describe as having many friends and then there is a closer inner circle and I'd say there were probably about two or three other young people in his year group that were particularly close with Kevin. But he was always very popular, very charming as well with the ladies, so you'd see him out and about on the playground; he'd be surrounded by children all the time.

Interviewer: That's nice to hear. We're interested in his status and when he was briefly not in education, employment, or training. That is why he's part of the project. What do you recall about his motivation for anything like employment or further education when he was at school? How would you describe him? Where was he kind of pointing towards?

Inclusion Manager: His ambition has always, always, been that he wants to do sports; that is his burning desire. We had many conversations before he left in Year 11 about what he would like to do when he left school. We discussed briefly him coming back to the sixth form at James Hill and he toyed with the idea for a while. But I think he was concerned that he would have the same level of staff breathing down his neck that he had previously and the other issue that influenced that was the fact that he wanted to get a job, he only wanted a little part-time job; if he asked me how to get a job at McDonald's once, he asked me 50 times! He said he just wanted a little job to earn some money because he wanted to continue his sports training, that was his main ambition and there was no talking him round that.

Interviewer: OK – that's nice that he had some kind of ambition. You touched on the fact that there were behaviour issues at school. Erm, did they go right the way through schooling? Was it just Year 7 or did it get worse towards Year 11? How did that pan out?

Inclusion Manager: He sort of followed the trend, actually, of a lot of our young men; he started off OK – as I said petty misdemeanours, nothing too terrible. As he sort of careered towards Years 9 and 10, erm, we started to see an increase in the amount of incidents that he was involved in and an increase in the severity of the incidents as well. It was at that point that we decided, obviously, that he needed to come onto our alternative provision and pretty much be educated up in the Centre of Inclusion. Obviously we still supported him with his options that he wanted to do and we made sure that he was still able to go and do the subjects that he was succeeding at. But for his core subjects he stayed with us and he coped really well with that. Towards Year 11 there was a massive improvement in his behaviour – and again, that sort of fits the norm. They sort of grow up between 14 and 15 and he certainly did; he did a lot of growing up in that time. We went from having two or three incidents a week to, I would say, probably in the last year only about three or four incidents throughout the entire year. So, yeah, his behaviour improved dramatically and I think that a lot of that's down to the focus that the sports gave him as well: there was a lot of drive and ambition there.

Interviewer: What were his basic skills like?

Inclusion Manager: Poor – his academic ability was very poor; obviously he was on the SEN register. I taught him English in the last two years and it was a real struggle; he was only, I'd say, about Level 3 English. So obviously he used to become very disheartened because he was painfully aware that his English wasn't fantastic and it was a struggle to keep him buoyed and enthusiastic when it came to his English coursework or any subject for that matter. Obviously the written content used to scare him and I think he would back away from it and make excuses. Maths was better, again following the norm; he seemed much more confident with his maths, much more comfortable. But still I wouldn't say that there was a burning desire for him to continue with maths or English when he left school. I think he acknowledged that's not where his strengths lay and obviously he just tolerated it – I'd say tolerated is probably the best word – by the end.

Interviewer: Did he ever get in trouble with the police?

Inclusion Manager: Yes. There were one or two incidents that I can recall: there was a theft and I know that there was an arson attempt as well, somewhere along the line. And I'm also aware that his relationship with his older brother often led him into lots of trouble as well; there were incidents where they'd been stopped in cars by police and the police would come in and want to speak to him in school. And actually I was quite pleased about that because we've got quite a nice relationship with the police and they come in and they do a lot of therapeutic stuff in school that actually meant that when Kevin was approached out of school by any police officers, he didn't have the reaction that perhaps a lot of other young people do. This was mainly because he was able to call them by name and they were able to call him by name. So I can remember the one time he was stopped in a car with his brother, neither of them actually old enough to drive and the police actually rang me and said that the boys had been very sensible and very calm about the whole issue and I was really pleased about that. But I'd say incidents, for him, getting himself into trouble; the last year, again, he stayed pretty much out of bother. He was very much a sort of Year 9 and Year 10, 13 and 14-year-old prankster more than anything else.

Interviewer: What was his attendance like?

Inclusion Manager: His attendance was a bit hit-and-miss; we went through a phase where he wasn't really coming in and we were quite concerned about where he was and what he was doing. Obviously we'd contact home and Mom would say "Well, he's left," and there were issues about where he was going and where he was meandering around of a daytime. That seemed to sort itself out; he seemed to give himself a bit of talking to or someone else did and whoever did, I'd like to thank them. Because then he started to come in and his attendance actually, in the last year I think if it wasn't a 100 per cent it was pretty damn close. He seemed to – while he didn't enjoy the academic element of school, he enjoyed the social, and as I've said he was a very popular young man and he seemed to come in even if just to socialize and nothing else. So yes – in the end his attendance did improve significantly.

Interviewer: Is there anything else you'd like to remember?

Inclusion Manager: Erm, I can say Kevin is one of these young people that, you know, you will remember for a very long time – mainly because I'm very proud of him, more than anything else. It's difficult with his home life and his background meant that he could have so easily fallen by the wayside and allowed himself to get into further mischief. Obviously the situation with his older brother as well has had a huge impact on how he's managing his own behaviour. Erm, I'm just immensely proud of Kevin. I'm proud of his achievements and I'm proud of the academic skills that he actually – I think he surprised himself when he opened his GCSEs with what he'd gotten and when we discussed and went over everything that he'd managed to get, he was genuinely really pleased and I think he was just a little taken aback. He was a very loving kid, very generous, a very big heart; and if I was ever having a day where I was struggling he'd come over and ask, "Is there anything you need?" – and very, very caring in that respect. As I mentioned, I saw him on the bus not long ago and the first thing was that I had a hug off him and a "Sit down with me and all my friends;" there was no embarrassment about who I was. He's just – he's a bit of trendsetter; people do tend to follow what he does and look to him to see what he's up to. I think Kevin is one of these young people who will stay with me for a very long time.

Connexions personal adviser's story

Interviewer: Tell me bit about Kevin and what he was like at school.

Personal Adviser: Ok, erm, Kevin – I saw Kevin initially in Year 10 in the summer, he was flagged up as somebody who would need extra support in terms of our intervention and extra guidance on his future. So I met him in Year 10 and we briefly talked about what his future ideas were and what he was very interested in. Well, he's an athlete, basically – and training to become an Olympian in the near future, so he talked a lot about that; very polite young man. He seemed quite focused on going into the uniform services and we looked at progression and what he needed to do to go into that. He wasn't really… I mean I wasn't… He was highlighted to me due to his, erm, LDD support that he needed in school, but he wouldn't and didn't like to talk about that very much. He was more focused on what he was going to need to do in terms of getting into the fire service and possibly wasn't that interested in the academic side of the support he needed in school. So I did have to challenge him a little bit about that.

Interviewer: You mentioned there about his learning difficulties and that he didn't like to talk about it. What sort of support did he need?

Personal Adviser: With the written work – numeracy and literacy basically. It wasn't a discrete… he wasn't following the normal curriculum, so he was doing the COPE award and going out on extended work experience. So he was in a smaller, discrete SEN group but he was School Action Plus for behavioural issues in school. When we talked about that, a lot of the time we spoke he would say it was possibly due to arguing with teachers a lot, sort of back-chatting, answering back and taking exception to what they said about him. But on the whole the feedback was that he's very polite.

Interviewer: You said he'd sometimes have problems with members of staff. Erm, did what sort of punishments (if you like) did he get?

Personal Adviser: I think it was sort of being told to leave the room, that sort of thing, possibly because in this particular school there is an area called Cape. It's an isolation area so a lot of the times he would spend his time in Cape where he would sort of be taken out and do his lessons there.

Interviewer: OK, so in isolation?

Personal Adviser: Yeah, in isolation [laughs].

Interviewer: OK. So did you know anything about his family at all?

Personal Adviser: Not really. I think he lived with his mom but that's the most I know about him.

Interviewer: OK. Particularly in Year 11 did he come to school every day?

Personal Adviser: I'm not sure about his attendance; it wasn't flagged up as being a particular issue – there might be issues with punctuality so he might be late but he comes into school, though I don't think he always comes in for registration. So that's probably why he did miss appointments because he never got his appointment slip in registration time so I missed him in school. I would have to just catch up with him in a corridor somewhere.

Interviewer: So he's hard to get hold of?

Personal Adviser: Yeah, he was hard to get hold of, yeah.

Interviewer: And if you were to describe the main support that you provided at school, what would you say that was?

Personal Adviser: I think, for me, it was – I found that he was positive and he said the right things but it was the fact that he didn't take action on what he needed to do. And it was sort of pinning him down to, "Have you applied to college yet? Have you done what you were supposed to do?" I mean, you know, in terms of his confidence it was all there, I mean, he was offered a part-time job working at a gym. He was doing voluntary work at a gym and he said they'd offered him a job so I wasn't worried about that. But in terms of his post-16 options, every time I spoke to him he hadn't done anything so I pinned him down to, like, "Look, we're going to fill in this application form." So it was that kind of thing.

Interviewer: And when you did pin him down and work with him, did he go through it with you OK?

Personal Adviser: Yeah, he was fine but I think in the end he didn't go to where we applied to initially but he was fine when we sat down together.

Interviewer: OK. And when he did leave school do you know what he went on to do?

Personal Adviser: He applied to college but when I did my regular follow-up he was offered a place back at sixth form and then as far as I was aware he was going back to sixth form but…

Interviewer: But he didn't turn up?

Personal Adviser: No, he didn't turn up.

Interviewer: I know you said that you thought he might live with Mom. Do you know anything about his home background?

Personal Adviser: No, I don't. I mean, I know he came here from the Caribbean, possibly in junior school; he wasn't born here – he was Jamaican. I mean, he's still got a little bit of an accent – a Jamaican accent when you speak to him – but nothing else.

Analysis of citations	
Changes in accommodation	4
References to low basic skills	6
Low motivation	3
Unemployment in family	1
Poor behaviour in school	15
LDD (receiving support)	3
Known to youth offending team	2
Poor school attendance	5

Chapter 11

Conclusions

We began this book with an appreciation of the negative outcomes for young people who are NEET and looked at some less considered features such as the continuance of intergenerational poverty. In doing so, we suggested that the phenomenon is linked to other adverse situations such as poor mental health, social exclusion, and those stemming from the impact of chaotic lifestyles.

From there we examined the assumptions about the duration and nature of childhood and how such ideas have developed and changed throughout history. We noted that our concerns about young people serve to extend the duration of childhood and allow systems to help them in ways that previous generations would not have imagined.

We then described the history of employment, looking in particular at the nature of work and how it has changed over time. In chapter 4 we described a way of identifying young people at risk of entering the NEET category by using locally developed screening tools. Such work confirmed that those most at risk have complex social circumstances and many sources of instability. To help prevent them from entering the category, we emphasize the importance of early identification, particularly for those who are especially vulnerable.

Finally we presented the accounts of five young people who were NEET at one point and have since progressed. We developed their stories by incorporating the perspectives of the key figures they had been closely involved with.

Nature of the sample

In presenting these case studies we do not claim robust sampling methods. The young people whose lives we have described were chosen from a list of 17- to 19-year-olds in the NEET category. However, the practicalities of gaining access to key people meant other factors became significant. A number of families with young people who were NEET were either unwilling to share their stories or had moved away, having severed all links with any officials including housing officers, schools, colleges, and job centre staff. Many families were leading unstable lives and were very suspicious of any contact with adults they did not know. Finding willing young people and their families was often facilitated by contacts through people they already knew who tended to be Connexions staff.

While we can only speculate on why those families did not want to engage in our study, it was fairly evident that they might have been involved in activities that, if disclosed, would lead to unwelcome encounters with other authorities. Their resistance might have also been connected to past involvements or experiences with officials or people they perceived as a threat.

Our case study participants shared a further common factor: they were all willing to take part. Other studies may uncover additional factors and situations that are relevant to young people ending up NEET. So while we have attempted to present a variety of case studies that we hope represent a cross-section of those in this category, we recognize the limitations of our method.

That said, the case studies highlight a variety of settings for NEET young people. While the factors identified by the screening tools might suggest some common features, each person's situation and experience are, to a certain extent, unique. A summary of the risk factors and citations is presented below.

Nature of risk factors

Each case study participant had a high risk-factor score and would have been involved in an early intervention project had one been available. They all had complex and chaotic lives, albeit in different ways.

Despite having the highest risk-factor score, as his account makes evident, Kevin clearly had ambition. The lack of a clear trajectory led him to be categorized as NEET for some time. It wasn't until his school teacher identified his talent for athletics and his sports mentors gave him the necessary support that he was able to gain enough stability to commit to a positive focus for the future. Tim's stability, similarly, was affected by a family break-up and caused a negative change in his behaviour that was clearly documented in the school's recollection of him. Unlike Kevin, however, Tim did not receive an intervention that might have helped him determine a distinct career path. While he was keen to work with cars, failing to secure a placement dented that particular ambition, leaving Tim feeling dejected and reluctant to place himself in situations that could lead to further rejection. Such factors caused him to remain in the NEET category.

Table 11.1: Risk factors and citations for case studies

Risk factor	Wayne		Emma		Kevin		Tim		Mia	
	Score	Citations	Score	Citations	Score	Citations	Score	Citations	Score	Citations
Accommodation	0		3	17	3	4	0	0	0	1
Low motivation	3	21	3	7	3	3	3	6	3	7
Behaviour issues	2	24	2	21	2	15	2	7	2	21
Unemployment in family	2	1	2	2	2	1	2	2	2	2
Poor basic skills	2	12	0		2	6	0	1	2	3
Known to YOT	0		0		1	2	1	4	0	3
Attendance < 80%	0		1	16	1	5	1	9	1	3
LDD	1	8	0		1	3	1	1	1	1
Totals	10	66	11	63	15	39	10	30	11	41

Also relevant to Tim's NEET status was his role within the house supporting his father, whose wife left the family home a couple of years ago. Tim's father does not have regular work but involves Tim when he can. Though Dad claims to feed and look after him, which undoubtedly provides Tim with some stability, their current relationship is not conducive to his progression into education, employment, or training.

Mia, Gemma, and Wayne all experienced teenage pregnancy. As chapter 1 outlined, in some areas, looking after a child is recognized as work. Among the three case studies there were significant differences. Gemma's relationship with the baby's father developed at a time when things were unstable at home with her mom. Mom describes herself as having "lost them" for five years and of wanting to spend time with them when they returned to live with her. Losing Gemma, by her own admission, "had an impact on school in a way, I think".

Gemma also highlights: "It's just that Mom went from obviously not telling me I had to go to school and then, like, all of a sudden trying to make me go to school." The change caused upset and was inconsistent with what Gemma was used to, and this led her to leave home while she was still at school. Gemma's attendance levels were particularly low as her stability was found through her boyfriend, who didn't attend either. After becoming a teenage mom and regaining contact with her, Gemma now sees her role as being a caregiver to her own family.

Mia, by contrast, was involved with a boy who tragically died of cancer as a teenager. The loss deeply affected Mia and her coping strategies invariably led her into the NEET category. With the support of Connexions, however, she started focusing on her future and exploring her interests. Though now pregnant, she is actively considering an alternative future for herself, one in which she re-engages with work.

Mia reached this stage following quite an intensive intervention that included regular one-to-one appointments and support to gain entry onto a training course. This poses the question of whether the amount of support Mia eventually required might have been reduced had she been identified early when she was facing tragedy in her life.

Wayne became a father at the end of Year 11. Having spent his school years struggling with basic skills and hanging around with a group of like-minded lads "who just wanted a laugh in the classroom regardless", he left school with very few qualifications. As his case study makes evident, however, his desire to gain a job was intensely pronounced – and was commented on by most of the people we interviewed. Following the birth of his son, Wayne has been especially motivated to gain employment. Though he initially required a wake-up call to ensure he attended interviews, his desire to provide for his own family and the necessary support from Connexions ensured that he has now successfully entered employment.

Complexity and instability

In chapter 1 we described the conditions needed for non-linearity (or chaos) to be a feature of people's lives. One is the absence of large-scale architectures or forces that can be interpreted as a young person lacking a credible and practical long-term plan. When considering post-statutory education, this absence is particularly relevant. Current legislation makes compulsory the attendance at a place of education until a person is 16. But following efforts to encourage involvement in some form of education or training until a person is 18, it is important to recognize that for those without a coherent long-term plan, it can be all too easy to disengage. Because there are no penalties for not engaging, many more young people may potentially be vulnerable to entering the NEET category.

Once they are disengaged, re-engaging is difficult. Tim has disengaged and has found some stability staying at home, sleeping late and helping his father from time to time. His experiences of rejection, combined with finding a positive role in the family, is unlikely to motivate him to seek training or employment in the near future.

So, when young people like Tim do enter the NEET category, how do we encourage them to re-engage and restore their levels of stability? First, they have to want to engage – although fortunately very few actively choose to be NEET, the majority simply lack the confidence and motivation to take the risk of engaging. Not all of them have a stable adult who can alleviate the impact of rejection. In Kevin's case, the adult was a sports teacher who gave him an opportunity to participate in an activity that built his commitment, confidence, and motivation. Provided with the financial support to facilitate this, Kevin excelled. Athletics gave him a focus in life that over time significantly shaped his future plans.

For people like Wayne, support came from organizations like Connexions, who identify what a person wants to do and ways to achieve those goals. Such organizations look at the different opportunities available and encourage young people to try them out. In Wayne's case, this meant phoning him to ensure he got out of bed and didn't miss an interview. Each individual will have their own barriers to a successful transition into education, employment, or training – and it is with support that these barriers can be overcome. However, support incurs a cost of time, money, and energy that could be significantly reduced if stability was established earlier.

As we discussed in chapter 2, the age that young people are considered to be adults – and thereby responsible for their own actions – has varied considerably throughout history. One danger for young people with chaotic lives is that as they get older, the statutory framework of education drops away and there is little to replace it. If we accept that non-linear development occurs in the absence of large-scale forces or architectures, we recognize the need for robust services that will provide long-term stability for the especially vulnerable. Stability includes sustained contact with professionals, since this is more conducive to developing the person's ability to trust – as Mia's account makes evident. Led to the local Connexions service following a re-awakened interest in a career, she was provided with the information she needed to re-engage.

Institutions and social exclusion

We have seen that the risk of entering the NEET category is higher among people who have been excluded from school or those at risk of being so. None of the case studies presented involved students who had been permanently excluded from secondary school, but this does not suggest that this group was ignored, simply that they were far harder to engage with. Those case studies we have presented, however, show that experiences of school were largely negative and leaving was seen more as a relief than a transition. Tim's description of school as being "horrible" is unlikely to see him return there in search of assistance, even if he wanted it. For those particularly vulnerable students, separating school from employment or training providers might continue to be an effective measure. Their school or academy may not be the first port of call should they wish to seek further help.

Such ideas are not new. Throughout history, marginalized and disabled groups have been rejected from mainstream societies but charitable organizations have offered assistance in the form of housing, work, role allocation, and treatment. These organizations are part of a long tradition of supporting such individuals and facilitating their inclusion. While most people who enter the NEET category would not consider themselves disabled, many are marginalized and have found themselves in situations that are misunderstood by others – as Mia and Gemma's case studies highlight. For those who have had a persecutory experience of education – despite their school's intentions – the availability of alternative institutions and individuals such as career officers or job centres might increase the likelihood of their engaging with education, employment, or training.

Benefits of early identification

Those who are NEET account for a minority of young people; most are affected by a range of destabilizing factors.

Getting disengaged young people to re-engage is time-consuming and expensive. The work we presented in chapter 4 suggests that more than half of those at risk of entering the NEET category can be identified by the age of 14 – which gives appropriate professionals time to acquire knowledge of the young person and their family situation. To develop the young person's trust is likely to be easier before disengagement with its associated poor attendance, difficult behaviour, and disagreements with staff has been entrenched. Screening for the risk factors that are relevant in a particular area is more conducive to early identification and would allow relevant professionals to start their work earlier and for resources to be targeted sooner for identified young people.

Targeting resources does not have to be a time-consuming activity: it might simply involve keeping an eye on an individual, ensuring you always say hello in the corridors, or ask how they are doing. With national figures indicating that each young person who is NEET costs the public purse £56,000 over the course of their lives (Lee and Wright, 2011), this additional attention seems a small price to pay for the successful transition to education, employment, or training. If early identification reduces the number, a further benefit – beyond improved outcomes for the people involved – will be a large saving.

In times of economic pressure, however, it is an uncomfortable truth that preventative services are especially vulnerable to cuts. It is easier to see the impact of putting out a fire in a house than it is to see that of smoke alarms being fitted in every home. It is reported, however, that of all the rescues the fire and rescue service attend, about 50,000 (140 a day) are in the home, killing nearly 500 and injuring more than 11,000. Many of these could have been prevented if people had an early warning and were able to get out in time. If a fire does break out in a house you are twice as likely to die if the house has no smoke alarm than in a house with such an alarm. The media turn high-octane rescue efforts into popular programmes and news stories, but very little is shown about services and campaigns that try to prevent such incidents, such as the targeted work that the police do in schools and with young people. A series about establishing Neighbourhood Watch schemes is just as unlikely to make it on to television screens. Yet analysis of data suggests that both smoke alarms and Neighbourhood Watch schemes offer excellent value for money (Department for Business, Innovation and Skills, 2009; Bennett *et al.*, 2008).

There is a real danger that preventative services will be lost because of a lack of transparent data. Screening provides a means of identifying vulnerable young people early and of generating data that will evidence its benefits. Being proactive rather than reactive, however, is a stance we have yet to see adopted. Using funds to develop screening tools to save money in the long term will be much better for the public purse than spending on the problem when it arises.

Confidence issues

Another overriding factor that emerged from our research was the importance of confidence to a person's risk of being NEET. Every case study participant presented several examples that highlighted their lack of confidence. This leads us to conclude that the risk factor we label "low motivation" is different from confidence. One particular example from Tim's case study was given by his father: "I think he's just getting depressed that he cor get a job – he wants a job but he cor get a job." Tim's stance might be seen as a method of avoidance owing to a continued fear of rejection, which might have contributed to a lack of confidence to do things for himself: "When he went to that job down at Kwik Fit, he got through to the, like, interview stage. They sent him a rail ticket to go down to sort himself out but I don't think he's got the confidence to go down on the train on his own."

Following the study described in this book, we looked further at the importance of confidence in relation to children we might have missed. Among this cohort were many who required some basic support because they lacked this trait. A similar number required support when completing an application form for a college course, as they "didn't want to get it wrong," or they "just want to double check it's OK". For many, this was the first time they had completed an application, so they often just wanted a person to be there to guide them through it; some simply didn't know where to start while others struggled to present their personal skills and achievements.

Our cohort highlighted that it is mostly young women who need this type of support. Having poor basic skills was not the prerequisite, however; those with high academic ability were equally vulnerable. Such individuals needed to know that the form was fully completed to reassure them that they had the best chance of receiving an offer of a college place. When faced with tasks of this nature, the support of an adult is especially beneficial. Confidence can be gained from home, school, and a range of different sources as long as the adult is someone they can trust. They can be either internal to school e.g. a teacher or external e.g. a Connexions personal adviser. Our research highlights this factor as requiring further investigation.

Attachment and trust

The role of a Connexions personal adviser involves engaging with young people, many of whom have had negative experiences of education and who might be distrustful of adults – even those employed to assist them. Building up trust is not straightforward, as a young person we will call Debbie illustrates. Debbie's Connexions personal adviser worked closely with her over a period of time. Debbie had poor attendance due to a medical condition and often required support with getting to school. Her confidence and self-esteem were low and her academic studies suffered accordingly. To overcome the barriers Debbie presented, her Connexions personal adviser spent time gaining her trust and learning about her condition and its effect on her. After identifying suitable provision and ensuring that appropriate measures met her specific needs, Debbie made a successful transition onto a training programme.

Debbie remained on the training programme for six months until a problem arose. She returned to Connexions and would only see the Connexions personal adviser she had worked with previously. Other advisers were available but Debbie refused to talk to anyone else. By working with the same Connexions personal adviser and explaining exactly what had happened, alternative provision was put in place. We suggest that only when they had a trusting relationship with a responsible adult can this type of progress be expected from a young person. Attachment theory – and its associated concepts – might therefore constitute a useful framework to develop ideas about the role the relationship plays. Whatever approach is considered, however, most professionals working with vulnerable young people recognize the importance of developing a trusting relationship, particularly with those at risk of entering the NEET category.

Redefining NEET

The current allocation of the term NEET is based on assumptions about the nature of employment that may benefit from a re-examination. In chapter 3 we surveyed the changing nature of employment and suggested that new developments in the nature of work might need to be incorporated into planning. After a number of anomalies are remedied, the first step in the process would be to recognize the difference between a *purposeful activity* and *formal employment or training*. For example, Kevin was assigned the NEET label because he was not in formal education or training. Yet his ambition regarding athletics is as healthy and motivating and his training schedule as disciplined as any employment-based work.

The second step relates to teenage parenthood that features in many accounts of those who are, or were, NEET. Mia is currently pregnant and thinking about what options she has. She would like to continue her education to try to gain more qualifications and develop her skills. For some young parents, the availability of childcare within the family makes it possible to continue work or training outside the home; for others, there is little or no support. If Mia is successful in gaining a college place or an apprenticeship, even if it is only part-time, she will not be classed as NEET.

For Gemma, meanwhile, who has two young children and is choosing to look after them at home while her partner looks for work, the British government might classify her as NEET. However, in other countries, as examples have shown, her decision to be a parent and primary carer to her children would be recognized as the equivalent of having a full-time job.

A third development that warrants consideration is the rise of voluntary activities and unpaid internships being classed as NEET. This has a negative connotation, even when young people are working towards something positive. For those who wish to enter certain jobs and industries, prior experience is often required. Teaching and the police service are two good examples.

While pre-entry experience is not a prerequisite for those wanting to become a police officer, when only 75 per cent of applicants make it through the first stage of the application, it is advantageous to have some experience of working with individuals or groups in the community – for example as a sports coach or local youth worker. Other useful voluntary experience might be as a volunteer police cadet, community support worker, or special constable.

Entry into teaching degrees also requires applicants to have experience. For example, Newman University, Birmingham, requests "recent and relevant school experience in a British state school with the required age group". The University of Worcester states that "candidates will be expected to have had some recent experience in a primary school setting and to include this as part of the supporting statement in their application. Currently, candidates, as a condition of entry, have to provide a report from a primary school headteacher after they have completed a minimum of two weeks' work experience."

For those who have such careers in mind, taking a year out after school to gain as much relevant experience as possible would be worthwhile and necessary. Yet even if they were successful in securing such placements – competition for volunteer positions is extremely fierce and very few young people are offered such opportunities – their undeniable achievement would ironically be discredited by the fact that they would still be classified as not in education, employment, or training.

Still other students are in unique situations that require them to remain in the NEET category. Some act as carers, some have opportunities to travel, while others might be supported by their parents as they pursue a sporting career, for example. For the time it takes to secure sponsorship deals and develop the performance level required to become professional, that young person would be classed as NEET.

These considerations aside, issues relating to young people who disengage from being economically active when they leave formal education still require attention and solutions. Life outcomes for this group are poor, as we discussed in chapter 1. Research has illustrated the link between experience of employment and breaking cycles of long-term intergenerational poverty. This book has tried to illuminate certain realities surrounding the transition between childhood and adulthood for some of society's particularly vulnerable young people. While there are questions and challenges pertaining to the way we conceptualize NEET, there is no doubt that if we can avoid an individual entering this category in the first place, their long-term future stands to benefit. If we fail in this endeavour, the efforts required to help them re-engage are not to be underestimated. Preventing the most vulnerable from entering this category is surely worthwhile, and will be aided by early identification by professionals with relevant skills and knowledge taking a compassionate and non-judgemental approach to their work.

Conclusion

We have examined the journeys of vulnerable young people as they make the difficult transition between childhood – defined by the state as dictating the need for education – and adulthood, defined as greater autonomy and self-determination. We have found that those most likely to disengage with education, employment, or training often have difficult and chaotic lives. Such people often generate coping strategies that can have an adverse impact on their long-term future, but with services to support them through these difficult transitions we hope to see the safe arrivals we are all striving for.

References

Aries, P. (1960) *Centuries of Childhood*. London: Random House.

Arnold, C. (2008) 'We am NEET'. Presentation made to BPS/DECP conference, Bournemouth, January.

Arnold, C. and Aparicio, A. (2010) 'Developing a local NEET screening tool'. Presentation made to Capita NEET conference, London, April.

Arnold, C. and Baker, T. (2011) 'Developing a NEET screening tool'. *Selection and Development Review*. Leicester: BPS publications.

Arnold, C., Emery, B., Hughes, D., and Travell, C. (1995) 'Predicting and preventing poor attendance in an urban comprehensive school: A computer-assisted approach'. *Pastoral Care in Education,* 13 (4), 24–8.

Arnold, C., Yeomans, J., and Simpson, S. (2009) *Excluded from School: Complex discourses and psychological perspectives*. Stoke on Trent: Trentham.

Audit Commission (2010) 'Against the Odds: Re-engaging Young People in Education, Employment or Training'. Online. www.audit-commission.gov.uk/SiteCollectionDocuments/Downloads/20100707-againsttheoddsfull.pdf (accessed 13 October 2011).

BBC (2009) 'Students at Home to Cut Costs'. Online. http://news.bbc.co.uk/1/hi/education/7972586.stm (accessed 29 August 2011).

Bennett, T., Holloway, K., and Farrington, D. (2008) *The Effectiveness of Neighbourhood Watch*. Glamorgan: The Campbell Collaboration.

British Educational Research Association (2004) *Revised Ethical Guidelines for Research*. Nottingham: British Educational Research Association.

British Psychological Society (2004) *Guidelines for Minimum Standards of Ethical Approval in Psychological Research*. Leicester: British Psychological Society.

Burt, C. (1927) *The Young Delinquent*. London: University of London Press.

Bynner, J. and Parsons, S. (2002) 'Social exclusion and the transition from school to work: The case of young people not in education, employment, or training'. *Journal of Vocational Behavior*, 60, 289–309.

Connell, M. (1991) *Against a Peacock Sky*. London: Penguin Books.

Cunningham, H. (2006). *The Invention of Childhood*. London: BBC Books.

Darlington, H.S. (1931) 'Ceremonial behaviourism: Sacrifices for the foundations of houses'. *The Psychoanalytical Review*, 18, 306–28.

deMause, L. (1974) *The History of Childhood*. London: The Souvenir Press.

Denscome, M. (2003) *Good Research Guide: For small scale research projects*. Berkshire: McGraw Hill.

Department for Business, Innovation and Skills (2009) 'A statistical report to investigate the effectiveness of the furniture and furnishing (fire) (safety) regulations'. London, 1988.

Donkin, R. (2010) *The History of Work*. Basingstoke: Palgrave Macmillan.

Dunbar, R. (1993) 'Coevolution of neocortex as a constraint on group processes'. *Behavioural Brain Science*, 16, 681–735.

— (2003) 'The social brain: Mind, language, and society in evolutionary perspective'. *Annual Review of Anthropology,* 32, 163–81.

Dyson, S. (2005) *Social Theory and Applied Health Research*. Berkshire: McGraw Hill.

Franzen, E.M. and Kassman, A. (2005) 'Longer-term labour-market consequences of economic activity during young adulthood: A Swedish national cohort study'. *Journal of Youth Studies*, 8 (4), 403–24.

Galbi, D. (1994) 'Child labor and the division of labor in the early English cotton mills'. *Journal of Population Economics*, 10, 357–75.

Giorgi, A. (1994) 'A phenomenological perspective on certain qualitative research methods'. *Journal of Phenomenological Psychology* 25 (2), 190-220.

Green, A. and White, R. (2008) 'Shaped by place: young people's decisions about education, training and work'. *Benefits*, 16 (3), 213–24.

Groenewald, T. (2004) 'A phenomenological research design illustrated'. *International Journal of Qualitative Methods*, 3 (1), Article 4. Online. www.ualberta.ca/~iiqm/backissues/3_1/pdf/groenewald.pdf (accessed 2 November 2008).

Health and Social Care Information Centre (2011) *Health Survey for England - 2011*. Leeds: Health and Social Care Information Centre.

Heidegger, M. (1927) *Sein und Zeit*. Halle: Niemeyer. Translated as *Being and Time* by John Macquarrie and Edward Robinson. Oxford: Blackwell, 1978.

Heywood, C. (2001) *A History of Childhood*. Cambridge: Polity Press.

Hicks, J. and Allen, G. (1999) *A Century of Change: Trends in UK statistics since 1900*. London: House of Commons Library.

Holmes, T. and Rahe, R. (1967) 'The social readjustment rating scale'. *Journal of Psychosomatic Research*, 11 (2), 213–18.

Husserl, E. (1936) *Die Krisis der europäischen Wissenschaften und die transzentale Phänomenologie: Eine Einleitung in die phänomenologische Philosophie (The Crisis of European Sciences and Transcendental Phenomenology: An introduction to phenomenological philosophy)*. Translated by David Carr (1970). Evanston, IL: Northwestern University Press.

Kim, S. (2007) 'Immigration, Industrial Revolution and Urban Growth in the United States, 1820–1920: Factor endowments, technology and geography'. Online. www.nber.org/papers/w12900 (accessed September 2011).

Lee, N. and Wright, J. (2011) *Off the Map?: The geography of NEETs*. Lancaster University: Private Equity Foundation.

Levering, B. (2006) 'Epistemological issues in phenomenological research: How authoritative are people's accounts of their own perceptions?'. *Journal of Philosophy of Education*, 40 (4), 451–62.

Lopez, K.A. and Willis, D.G. (2004) 'Descriptive versus interpretive phenomenology: Their contribution to nursing knowledge'. *Qualitative Health Research*, 14 (5), 726–35.

LSN (2009) *Tackling the NEETs problem: Supporting local authorities in reducing young people not in employment, education, and training*. London: LSN.

Mazur, A. (1973) 'A cross-species comparison of status in small established groups'. *American Sociological Review*, 38, 513–30.

Maguire, S. and Rennison, J. (2005) 'Two years on: The destinations of young people who are not in education, employment, or training at 16'. *Journal of Youth Studies*, 8 (2) 187–201.

Miller, R.L. and Brewer, J.D. (eds) (2003) *The A–Z of Social Research*. London: Sage Publications.

Morris, D. (1990) *Animal Watching: A field guide to animal behaviour*. London: Jonathan Cape.

NCH (2007) *Literature Review: Resilience in children and young people*. London: NCH.

Office for National Statistics (2011) *Health Statistics Quarterly*, 49 (spring). Online. www.ons.gov.uk/ons/rel/hsq/health-statistics-quarterly/spring-2011/index.html (accessed 3 March 2012).

O'Rourke, K. and Williamson, J. (1999) *Globalisation and History: The evolution of a nineteenth-century Atlantic economy*. Boston: MIT.

Patton, W. and McMahon, M. (2001) *Career Development Programs: Preparation for lifelong career decision making*. Melbourne: Acer Press.

Pawson, R. and Tilley, N. (1997) *Realistic Evaluation*. London: Sage.

Pemberton, S. (2007) 'Tackling the NEET generation and the ability of policy to generate a "NEET" solution – evidence from the UK'. *Environment and Planning C: Government and Policy*, 26, 243–59.

— (2008) 'Social inclusion and the "get heard" process'. *Public Policy and Administration*, 23 (2), 127–43.

Peters, T. (1985) *Thriving on Chaos: Handbook for a management revolution* London: Harper Books.

Pitchford, M. (2006) Secondary School Action Plan (personal communication).

Postman, N. (1994) *The Disappearance of Childhood*. New York: Vintage Books.

Robson, K. (2008) 'Becoming NEET in Europe: A comparison of predictors and later-life outcomes'. Paper presented at the Global Network on Inequality Mini-conference, New York City, 22 February.

Ross, L. (1977) 'The intuitive psychologist and his shortcomings: Distortions in the attribution process'. In Berkowitz, L. (ed.) *Advances in Experimental Social Psychology*, 10. New York: Academic Press.

Selbye Bigge, L.A. (1924) *Psychological Tests of Educable Capacity*. London: HMSO.

Simmons, R. (2008) 'Raising the age of compulsory education in England: a NEET solution?'. *British Journal of Educational Studies*, 56 (4), 420–39.

Social Exclusion Unit (1999) *Bridging the Gap: New opportunities for 16–18 year olds not in education, employment, or training*. Cm 4405, Social Exclusion Unit, London: HMSO.

Spielhofer, T., Marson-Smith, H., and Evans, K. (2009) 'Non-formal Learning: Good Practice in Re-engaging Young People Who Are NEET'. Online. www.voced.edu.au/content/ngv16026 (accessed 29 May 2009).

Sprenkle, D.H. (2005) *Research Methods in Family Therapy*. New York: Guilford Publications Inc.

Stubblefield, C. and Murray, R. (2002) 'A phenomenological framework for psychiatric nursing research'. *Archives of Psychiatric Nursing*, 16 (4), 149–55.

Sukkoo, Kim (2007) 'Immigration, Industrial Revolution and Urban Growth in the United States, 1820-1920: Factor endowments, technology and geography'. NBER Working Paper no. 12900. Cambridge, MA: National Bureau of Economic Research.

Super, D.E. (1954). 'Career patterns as a basis for vocational counselling'. *Journal of Counselling Psychology*, 1, 12–20.

Syke, E. (2010) 'Ofsted, exclusion, and massaging data: A vicious trio'. *Race Equality Teaching*, 28 (3), 21–4.

Uzuki, Y. (2010) *Intergenerational Persistence of Poverty in the UK*. London: Centre for Analysis of Social Exclusion, Annual Report 68.

Vallois, H. (1961) 'The social life of early man: the evidence of skeletons'. In *Social Life of Early Man*, Sherwood, L., Washborne (ed.) Chicago, cited in deMause, L. (1974).

Wagstaff, A. (2002) 'Poverty and health sector inequalities'. *Bulletin of the World Health Organization*, 80 (2), 97–105.

Walther, A. and Pohl, A. (2005). 'Thematic study on policy measures concerning disadvantaged youth'. Study commissioned by the European Commission: Final Report.

Wilson, S., Cunningham-Burley, S., Bancroft, S., and Backett-Milburn, K. (2008) 'Joined up thinking? Unsupported "fast-track" transitions in the context of parental substance abuse'. *Journal of Youth Studies*, 11 (3), 283–99.

Index